To Be a Man

To Be a Man

GEORGE DEVINE

*Editor of the Proceedings of the
College Theology Society*

Prentice-Hall, Inc., *Englewood Cliffs, New Jersey*

Nihil obstat:
Very Rev. Msgr. William F. Hogan
CENSOR LIBRORUM

Imprimatur:
✠ Most Rev. Thomas A. Boland, S.T.D.
ARCHIEPISCOPUS NOVARCENSIS

Newark, New Jersey, January 22, 1969

LIBRARY OF CONGRESS CATALOG CARD NO.: 69-20489
PRINTED IN THE UNITED STATES OF AMERICA

CURRENT PRINTING (LAST NUMBER):
10 9 8 7 6 5 4 3 2 1

PRENTICE-HALL INTERNATIONAL, INC., *London*
PRENTICE-HALL OF AUSTRALIA, PTY. LTD., *Sydney*
PRENTICE-HALL OF CANADA, LTD., *Toronto*
PRENTICE-HALL OF INDIA PRIVATE LTD., *New Delhi*
PRENTICE-HALL OF JAPAN, INC., *Tokyo*

Acknowledgments

The editor of this volume, himself a member of the College Theology Society and concerned with the vitality of that body, wishes to thank all of those within and outside of the Society who have contributed substantively to the successful publication of this volume of the Society's annual Proceedings.

The book could not have appeared had it not been for the confidence and encouragement which the editor received from the Board of Directors of the Society, especially our president, Rev. Mark Heath, O.P.; our secretary, Sister Maura Campbell, O.P.; our treasurer, Brother C. Stephen Sullivan, F.S.C.; and also in a special way Rev. Albert J. Zabala, S.J. Particular thanks must go to the previous Proceedings editor, Sister Katharine T. Hargrove, R.S.C.J., who not only established an admirable standard of excellence for the publication but also gave much valuable advice to the present editor.

Needless to say, gratitude is expressed to all of the contributors to the book, but the editor would like to single out those additional authors who did not speak at the 1968 Annual Convention in San Francisco and whose articles give testimony to the ongoing dynamism of our theological endeavors: Professor Vincent Zamoyta, Professor Peter G. Ahr, and Rev. Charles Kohli.

Several individuals were most helpful in giving critical reactions to the book, in part or in whole, at various stages of its formation. In this regard, thanks are especially due to Rev. Thomas Heath, O.P., Rev. Robert E. Hunt, Rev. William Driscoll, Mr. Peter M. Devine, and a number of the editor's students and colleagues at Seton Hall University.

The physical production of the book and its appearance are in the main due to the fine work of Prentice-Hall, Inc., particularly Mr. Paul O'Connell, and Miss Janice Medlock.

If one person is to be noted as contributing most significantly to the editor's efforts, it is certainly Miss Sally Abeles, whose amazing technical competence and charming patience made it a joy to work with her.

Lastly, the editor wishes to thank all those who have been around and with him throughout this task in so many ways, but most importantly his wife, Joanne.

GEORGE DEVINE

Contents

I Introduction

GEORGE DEVINE

1 Changes

Not long ago, at the university in which I teach, a group of students joined in a term project for an interdisciplinary course entitled "Psychotheology." Their task was to articulate in some way the religious or theological, the emotional, the psychological dimensions of the experiences of today's young people. They did it, not by means of a research thesis or a neatly typed essay, but in a movie.

The film showed the young people in action and reaction as they braced themselves for the crispness of autumn and sloshed through the snows of winter, as they frolicked among the trees and skated on the frozen pond. It made us in some way privy to their feelings as they stood atop the Jersey palisades gazing across the river at the bigness that is Manhattan, as they drove through the lonely slums of Newark and New York, and as they confronted police in a protest march. They let us share their experiences as they ran gleefully, sauntered ponderously, hugged, kissed, prayed, smiled, worried—and thought a lot about themselves and their world.

Throughout the otherwise silent cinema we heard the folksongs that have become so expressive of and for today's young people. The song heard most often is one called "Changes." That is the name of the film. And I suggest that it is the name of the game as far as young people and their teachers—especially teachers of theology—are concerned.

The present college generation is like all others in that it has to face and cope with a number of changes. It feels that it is *unlike* all others insofar as the changes it has to deal with are more widespread and manifold, more exciting and terrifying, more sudden and

3

stunning than the changes which have confronted any previous collegiate generation.

The college teacher or administrator, and especially one whose concern is with theology or religious education, cannot merely observe and evaluate the changes in dispassionate fashion, partly because they affect him too but also partly because in a very real way he is part of them, any alleged "generation gap" notwithstanding.

By and large, today's collegians see themselves as having been born in a time of secure smugness, just after World War II. America and her allies had triumphed over the Axis, and all other nations were manifestly inferior to Johnny when he came marching home again. The vaunted *Übermenschen* of pure Aryan strain had been beaten in the European theater, and the Japanese had been pounded to bits by the atom bomb, the ultimate weapon of devastation possessed only by Uncle Sam.

As Erich Fromm sarcastically said in *The Sane Society*, "Everybody's happy nowadays." That was the world into which today's collegians feel they were born. It is exceedingly different from the world which they face two decades later.

Even the fifties, in which our present students grew up, were to be remembered as the "placid decade." There had been Korea and the Soviet development of A- and H-bombs, but there was also the prevailing conviction that God was in His heaven and all was right with the world.

For those now in college, the security blanket didn't wear out until at least midway through the sixties. In fact, the earlier years of the decade were probably the most hopeful in a long time for people of any generation. As Martin Marty wrote in *America*, "Utopia was not wholly implausible. Pope John and President John, Saint Nikita and Reverend King would help take care of things; only mopping-up operations for the kingdom of God were ahead."[1]

Yes, as recently as a few years ago, Christians—perhaps more particularly Catholics—of all ages felt that they had reason to expect a Teilhardian convergence (whether they knew it by that name or not). The lines pointing to the Omega were seen to be like the plot lines of a Shakespearean play: even after apparent deviation or reversal, they all came home to roost.

Despite the agonies of the planet from Laos to Little Rock, it

[1] Martin Marty, "A Warning to Catholic Extremists," *America*, CXIX, no. 5 (August 31, 1968), 123.

took not too much visionary ability to see the Spirit brooding above the waters.

The Catholic Church that existed before and even during the Second Vatican Council fit well into the picture. Part of the whole operation of redemption was to be the internal reform of Christ's body on earth in an effective, harmonious, and glorious manner so as to make her even more obvious as the Way in which this redemption was to be facilitated.

Is the weltanschauung presented above far too simplistic? Perhaps. But it is one which was opted by a number of people—not only young people—in a time when disappointment seemed to be in retreat, however temporarily, and which provided a nice workable conclusion for the pros and cons of human experience in the previous decades. Man, it seemed, had not only put his finger on his deepest problems but was about to begin doing something about them, in a variety of spheres—international, political, economic, interracial, religious.

In the few years that have followed since that time, Vietnam, Watts, Czechoslovakia, Detroit, and Nigeria-Biafra have all made their impress on the human consciousness, as have the words and deeds of H. Rap Brown and James Farmer, Mayor Daley and Gene McCarthy and George Wallace, Pope Paul and Eduard Schillebeeckx and Cardinal O'Boyle. Most painfully, there were Dallas, Memphis, and Los Angeles.

The more experienced and sagacious citizens, confronted with these realities, have often been able to sigh heavily and put on the shelf the type of optimism of which Marty wrote. For the young people, though, the very history in which they grew up seems perhaps to represent a betrayal. They had all matured enough to know that the world seen by a child and the world seen by an adult are two different things. None of them, I am confident, expected adulthood to involve simply a continuous rerun of the "Ozzie and Harriet" placebos they had been exposed to on the boob tube.

But, I submit, today's collegians (and recent postcollegians, probably) have in many ways had the psychological, emotional, and spiritual rug yanked out from under them, and so have developed growing pains unlike those of other generations.

It is often said that one of the key areas—if not *the* key area— of this experience is that of international relations in a nuclear age. As noted above, the Bomb was a symbol of the *pax Americana* when our college students of today were small children. Now it is more properly—and at best—the symbol of a delicate balance, a sword of Damocles. Everyone now alive knows "crisis" as a household word, has lived through a "crisis" every year or so, and feels his pulse quicken when he hears the words, "We interrupt this broadcast. . . ." Our young people, it seems, feel an insecurity about living, despite their youth and vitality. It is an insecurity which is not from time immemorial but quite recent, and it is not of their own making. Perhaps (many have said this) it helps to account for their tremendous anxiety and impatience, their spirit—for good or ill—of *carpe diem*. They have an urgent desire to know what will make things right *today*, and a lack of patience for solutions that appear to be too long-range. This is something which, I think, has made them somewhat unsympathetic to the kind of patient faith which their elders would be more ready to accept naturally.

The changing racial situation in America, I submit, also plays a part in the matter, if for no other reason than this: As recently as five years ago, the average suburban white sympathetically repeated the right answers to the problems of bigotry and discrimination. Perhaps he went on the right march or held the right placard. Today, the Black Power movement has told him that he didn't have the answers after all, and that he would do well to take his placard and go elsewhere. The phenomenon is deeper than implied by the case in point; it involves the uncomfortable feeling of somewhat laboriously arriving at the answers to find out that they are not answers after all. It is a jarring experience indeed.

The previous point has much to do with the religious orientation —or lack of it—of today's young people. Remember that the students now in college were yet to enter during and right after Vatican II. Thus, they have been caught up in a peculiar set of circumstances as far as religious education is concerned. They have largely been products of a catechetical system which sincerely attempted to communicate wholly the faith life of Christ's Church, but which often seems to have made the mistake of articulating the accidental just (or almost) as forcefully as the substantial—Latin in the mass and no meat on Friday with the Blessed Trinity and the Virgin Birth.

I submit that those of us who are just a little older (now approaching the untrustworthy age of thirty!) were able to view and be involved in the conciliar *aggiornamento* in many of its dimensions from the enviable location of the undergraduate or graduate

theology classroom, and thus enjoyed a sense of gradual development, continuity, and perspective not so readily available to today's
collegians. They seem to have real difficulty in perceiving a *via
media* between total upheaval and no change at all. They may feel
personally threatened because the slightest jots and tittles have passed
away, or jubilant over the fact that some changes mean that "the lid
is off" and "anything goes";[2] more often, they may simply be confused and searching. In any case, the rug *has* been yanked out from
under them: they have felt the impact of change—in the Church
and elsewhere—in a way which shall be seen as different from the
experiences of either their elders or their juniors. From my own
campus experience, I can say that today's college students are quite
different in their needs and orientations from those of four years
ago, and I believe that they are indeed quite different from those
who will arrive in our colleges several years hence.

This volume represents the inner life of a scholarly community,
one of professors in the field of theology or religious studies. The
essays that follow are drawn mainly from papers read in April, 1968,
at the Fourteenth Annual Convention of the College Theology Society. It is our attempt herein, as it was last Easter week in San
Francisco, to engage in dialogue and self-examination, precisely in
terms of the existential needs and situations of those students whom
we serve. We may not always latch onto answers with arrogant
clarity, but perhaps we can more clearly discern and delineate some
important areas of question and implications for future directions.

As some of the authors point out, man thinks of himself today in
ways which are not identical with the ways of yesterday. Father
Faricy will demonstrate that the evolutionary images of Teilhard
de Chardin have made their mark here, and Professor Cobb will
treat of a new self-understanding of the Christian man in his psychic
dimensions.

This will give rise to new emphases of contemporaneity—a desire
to be with it in terms of today's world. Sister Anita highlights this.
And Professor Michaelsen notes a new sort of belief, a type which

---

[2] This, to my mind, involves a real hazard in a situational approach to
morality. One who misreads Augustine, as Joseph Fletcher seems to, by saying
that "love is the only measure" of the rightness or wrongness of a moral action
all too often neglects the question, "Is my action in this case an effective incarnation of genuine and responsible love?" In a rather amorphous moral
climate, the neglect of such an important question can and often does result
in many young people's being very sadly—and probably unnecessarily—hurt.

is perhaps less trustful of old formulas, yet more trustful of the very concept of belief itself . . . quite possibly the type of belief Professor Ahr speaks of.

Religious faith for today's young people will be more humanistic and ecumenically oriented than that of their predecessors, and this point will be explored by Professor Hutchison. It will involve a re-examination of that moving power which causes us to believe, namely, evidence, discussed by Professor Burke.

In all cases, we are talking—at least partially—in terms of the *fides* which is not mere intellectual assent, but a genuine faith *life*. Messrs. Cogley and Vaughn have their finger on the pulse of things, in describing possible dimensions for action in the religious experience of today's young people. They are a people anxious to act, yet often confused, as the differing views expressed by Professor Zamoyta and Father Wassmer will indicate.

In the last analysis, our effort at understanding our students is of its nature not only a complex one; it must also be a constant one. This is why the Proceedings volumes are not and cannot be gray, pedestrian reports of just what was said by a group of teachers to each other. The San Francisco convention itself was vital in its nature and broad in its spectrum. Making major contributions were not only the theologian but also the man versed in psychology, the journalist, the director of the Peace Corps.

So it is with this book. It does not merely rehearse the utterances of a past event but reflects the ongoing life of the theological profession in general and of our Society in particular. To this end, we have included three contributions (exclusive of this introduction) not delivered in San Francisco, all written since the ferment in the Church caused by but in no wise restricted to Paul VI's encyclical *Humanae vitae*. So it is that we have thoughtful and diverse reactions from two university professors, Peter Ahr and Vincent Zamoyta, and a sensitive homily by a former professor, Father Charles Kohli.

It is hoped that our profession and our Society will continue to be vital, and that this volume may serve that vitality in the classroom, the professional workshop, the study group. To this end is this book offered, that we may join our students in an understanding of human experience, of what it is *To Be a Man*, so that when the Word of God has become fully incarnate in the world, we may see the realization of the Christian vision that has inspired Father Kohli . . . mankind at one.

II Opening Observation

ROBERT MICHAELSEN

2 How Much Can
Today's College Student Believe?

When faced with the question of how much today's college student can believe, my initial response is: everything *and* nothing. I find skepticism of the old Humian variety or after the manner of Voltaire quiescent today. Lord Russell is admired more for his stand on Vietnam than for his attacks upon the Christian weltanschauung. Harvey Cox is right, I think, when he writes that Bertrand Russell's books often seem more quaint than daring today.

At the same time, credulity here and there raises its innocent-appearing head. I know students who are seriously interested in such things as alchemy, witchcraft, and satanism. And a little band of the faithful followers of one Indian seer (not Maharishi) confidently anticipated a major physical happening when this man broke his long-imposed silence; the mere uttering of the sacred word *om* might, it was thought, set up vibrations which would cause Southern California to float out to sea.

Faith also still lives among the student generation. But it does not often follow conventional forms. In fact, I do not know just what past categories to use in describing the mood of students today. This is neither an age of faith nor an age of reason. Perhaps it is the age of feeling. Perhaps we are on the edge of a new age of enthusiasm—in the literal sense of that word.

To ask *how much* the student can believe is to put the question in terms of past categories. It is to use the old quantifying approach: to be a Christian is to believe so and so much. It is something that can be measured on some kind of scale, by some divine calculus.

In my seminary days, we sometimes toyed with the question: how *little* can one believe and still be a Christian? How about the inerrancy of the Bible? The virgin birth? The miracle stories? The resurrection? The trinitarian formulation? I recall studies done among Protestant clergymen a generation and more ago which showed that "liberal" ministers almost all believed in God. But less than half believed in the virgin birth. And still fewer believed in hell.

This kind of arithmetic approach, however, is an old game which I suspect is significant today primarily and perhaps only to those hung up on the divine calculus, to those who are caught in the quantifying box. The question today is not *how much* or even *what* one can believe. It is how I can live, how I can be human.

I have suggested that this might be called an age of feeling rather than an age of faith or an age of reason. I am not among the adulators of Maharishi, but I think he had something going for him when he said, according to *Los Angeles Times* reporter Arthur J. Dommen, that the age of faith is gone. What has taken its place is experimentation, which Maharishi calls "the ideal of the present age." But this is experimentation in which one is involved himself, not a detached kind of tinkering with objects outside oneself. In fact, *involvement* is one of the key words, and one of the desired goals. On the campus of the University of California at Santa Barbara, where I teach, the most persistent reaction to the slaying of Martin Luther King, Jr., was summed up in the words, "What can I do?" This has become not only a poignant question but a platform for seeking meaningful involvement.

One of the most devastating criticisms leveled against the older generation is that we are not involved. We are, in the figure employed by Bob Dylan, thin men, or in the figure used by the earlier and more respectable poet T. S. Eliot, hollow men. Toward the end of Albert Camus' *The Stranger*, as Meursault, the protagonist, awaits his execution, he turns violently on the prison priest with the assertion that none of the priest's certainties was worth one strand of a woman's hair. This juxtaposition captures the difference between belief and experience and puts well a prevailing outlook today.

The songs of disenchantment with the fathers range from sad to strident, wistful to apocalyptic. But through them all runs the theme of the obtuseness and emptiness of the elders. Mr. Jones doesn't even know what's happening, let alone dig it. But "The times they are a-changin'," and "A hard day's rain is gonna fall." This lack of depth perception and communication is seen as hovering over all like a Los Angeles smog. Human relations are strained, foreshortened, ineffectual, and even meaningless. One pair of young bards, Simon and Garfunkel, see "Ten thousand people, maybe more, / People talking without speaking, / People hearing without listening. . . ."

So what is needed in the context of apparent emptiness? Belief? It seems like a dubious and ineffectual prescription. Faith? Perhaps in the sense of trust. But above all, experience.

Experience in love. How many song titles, be-ins, antiwar demonstrations, underground films created by young people have centered on the word *love?*

Experience of self—and beyond—in consciousness expansion. This through drugs, yes. But also through meditation. Three hundred and fifty Berkeley students signed up in the fall of 1967 for an experimental course in "Types of Meditation." At that same time, more than six hundred students at my campus were participating in transcendental meditation groups. There is a great fascination for the ways of the Eastern religions—meditation in Hinduism and Zen, for example. However, I see no serious reason that these same students might not become interested in the mystical tradition and techniques of the West. Perhaps the biggest problem stems from the fact that this tradition has not been greatly cultivated within the Christian community in the recent past.

Experience of life—especially the joyous, festive celebration of life. One who works on a California campus is continuously aware that there are in America today hordes of healthy, zesty youth. Half the population is below the age of twenty-five, and even though a few put on a long face and try to look anemic, the great mass is bursting with youthful energy. (It is enough to make an old man weary.) These bumptious youngsters dig life. They go for a religion which celebrates life, which helps them live.

At this point, as one of my colleagues put it, one might begin to see Baal coming out of the woods. Loving, blowing one's mind in consciousness expansion, celebrating life—all this might just add up to one big pagan ball of wax.

In any case, the Christian theologian has work to do. To understand and describe faith as intimately related to life. To talk about belief, if he talks about it at all, more in descriptive than in normative terms, realizing that words, while useful and necessary, must be related dialectically to experience. To point to exemplary models of human living, models which have the capacity to capture the imagination of youthful laymen. To affirm God in the midst of life. But that is hardly a new task for the Christian theologian.

III Images of Man

SISTER ANITA CASPARY, I.H.M.

3 The Self-Image of the Contemporary Young Adult

Rarely has any generation felt so strongly as do contemporary young adults that they constitute a community in themselves, existing separate and besieged right in the middle of an uncomprehending environment to which their very processes of awareness are alien and antithetical. And all of us over thirty (except for the few who can be trusted) are onlookers at this happening.

To speak of the self-image of the contemporary young adult demands a panel of well-trained sociologists, anthropologists, cultural historians, artists, and musicians, not to speak of college theology teachers. I am not at all qualified in any of these roles. Yet as fugitive from a college English department, then as college president and mother general, I can give you personal observations and conclusions supplemented by communication with Sister-students who are in touch on campuses from Berkeley and U.C.L.A. to Columbia, from Toronto to London.

To encapsulate this experience, I will look at *The Graduate*, a motion picture which, according to the reactions of young adults, presents an accurate image of them. There are perhaps few today who are familiar with Booth Tarkington's *Seventeen*, a drama gently satirizing the awkwardness of adolescents entering adulthood. *The Graduate* has no such charm of innocence; it is rather a black comedy in which Benjamin Braddock, home from college, is placed in a series of situations designed to initiate him into adult life.

Without hostility or sheer truculence, Benjamin is forced away from the adult world, a world in which the young seem much more serious than the old. The gap between the generations widens. Between the two groups are things

Like hypocrisy about sex—good for the parents in any and all forms but something to be kept away from the young. Like pretentiousness. Like self-aggrandizement masquerading as friendly fatherly advice. Like glad-handing instead of really liking somebody. Like talking man-to-man fairness but turning vicious when it's your ox that's gored. Like using people. These are things that everybody knows about and agrees about, to be sure. But—these kids are taking them seriously! [1]

A birthday party given by Benjamin's parents is symbolic of the conflict between the generations. The party takes place with the ubiquitous barbecue around the ubiquitous back-yard pool. Benjamin, clad in his new diving suit, is urged into the scene by his parents, who delight in their gift. From the depths of the suit he peers out, serious and embarrassed, at the playful frolic of his elders, unable to hear their voices, hearing only the exaggerated sound of his own breathing. He dives reluctantly into the pool and, sinking to its depths, remains gravely underwater, for the moment safe from the older generation, though alienated—"a rock, an island," as the folksingers have it.

David Brinkley, the news commentator, comments that young adults like this picture "because it said about parents and elders what *they* would have said if they had made the movie themselves—that we are self-centered and materialistic, that we are licentious and deeply hypocritical about it, that we try to make them into walking advertisements for our own affluence, our own vanities draped around their necks like garlands of rancid marigolds." [2]

The Graduate seems to sum it all up—the sense of dignity the young are trying to preserve by moving away from the absurd expectations of their elders; the respect they have for the buoyancy of hope, sometimes juxtaposed with a feeling of sharp despair; their willingness to scrap old patterns and symbols; their need for idealistic vision; their willingness, perhaps even their ability, to take responsibility for the world. Here, too, in *The Graduate* is the theme of the utter loneliness felt by the young, epitomized in "The Sound of Silence," which echoes through the picture:

> Hello, darkness, my old friend,
> I've come to talk with you again,
> Because a vision softly creeping

[1] Charles Burr, quoted on the cover of the Columbia soundtrack recording of *The Graduate*.
[2] David Brinkley, "Journal," *Ladies Home Journal*, April, 1968, p. 79.

Left its seeds while I was sleeping,
And the vision that was planted in my brain
Still remains
Within the sounds of silence.
In restless dreams I walked alone
The narrow streets of cobbled stone.
'Neath the halo of a street lamp,
I turned my collar to the cold and damp
When my eyes were stabbed by the flash
of the neon light
That split the night,
And touched the sounds of silence.
And in the naked night I saw
Ten thousand people, maybe more,
People talking without speaking,
People hearing without listening,
People writing songs that voices never shared.
No one dared
Disturb the sounds of silence.
Fools, said I, you do not know.
Silence like a cancer grows.
Hear my words that I might teach you,
Take my arms that I might reach you.
But my words like silent raindrops fell,
And echoed in the wells of silence,
and the people bowed and prayed
To the neon God they made.
And the sign flashed out its warning
In the words that it was forming,
And the sign said, the words of the prophets
Are written on the subway wall, the tenement halls,
And whispered in the sounds of silence.[3]

This theme of alienation is, of course, a powerful indictment of the Establishment, which creates nowhere men, gray-flannel-suit men, who can speak only a nonhuman language in a computerized world. The lyrics of "A Well-Respected Man" describe them:

He gets up in the morning
And he goes to work at nine,
And he comes back home at five-thirty,
Gets the same train every time
'Cause his world is built on punctuality. . . .
And he's oh, so good,

[3] From "The Sound of Silence" by Paul Simon, © 1964 by Charing Cross Music, used with permission of the publisher.

And he's oh, so fine,
And he's oh, so healthy in his body and his mind.
He's a well-respected man about town,
Doing the best things so conservatively. . . .[4]

The Graduate carries also a theme related to alienation: the desperate need for meaningful interpersonal relationships, for sharing and trust—the kind of reaching out to another human person which defies the automated, cybernetic, guided-missile world we live in. To this theme is linked a search for personal fulfillment, a kind of "Come Swing with Me" approach, a direct invitation to the dance of life, to do your thing, to go where the action is. Of course, this theme implies a deep criticism of the man or woman who has never "hung loose," who has bowed to convention and conformity and the performance principle and by that means has slowly died inside.

Likewise, *The Graduate* brings out the search of the contemporary young adult for raw experience, his concentration on the present moment and his scorn of formulas or dogmas which obscure the richness of life. Only in such experience, young people seem to say, is self-identity found.

The freedom sought by young adults is seen in their strong drive toward humanism, the values they place on human beings and human life. Their attitudes toward war are fairly obvious; so too are their attitudes toward racial or national barriers. In a student newspaper, a young movie critic quoted these lines from *Lonely Are the Brave* as the "most beautiful of all": "I don't believe in boundaries. Who sets up the separation, this is Texas and across that line is New Mexico and over there is Mexico? Who makes those borders? It's all the same, man." [5]

The protest in education made by contemporary young adults would seem not to arise simply from the democratization process by which the student wishes to be a partner in academic and administrative decisions. Also operative here, I think, is the humanistic principle, a distrust of mass production applied to persons, a fear of manipulation by the power structure, a desire for involvement and a search for relevance. Seriousness is again the pervasive atmosphere. A student admonished the faculty in a college newspaper in these words: ". . . the individual student expects to be taken seriously,

[4] From "A Well-Respected Man," © 1965 by Edward Kassner Music Co., Ltd., London, used with permission.
[5] *Comment* (Immaculate Heart College newspaper), March 18, 1968, p. 3.

and . . . being taken seriously means to the student that she be shown the relevance of a course of studies to her present—her present needs and her present environment." [6]

Beneath all the brave claims and honest demands, however, there lies a very real fear in the young adult. Another student in the same paper stated: ". . . these are hard times to be a student. Hard times that require courage—not that courage is a panacea. I don't mind admitting that this educational experience is terrifying. I am terrified by my own inertia, and [by] the opening and continuing recognition of the fact that all I once called sacred isn't." [7]

A subliminal common fear, a similarity of ideas and concerns, a desire for experience rather than theorizing about experience have created an international community of the young. Binding it together are deviations from accepted custom in dress and appearance, the development of an esoteric language, and involvement in the ritual of folksinging. The community has become for young adults their own "best defense against the aggressive incursions of the older people," [8] as well as the context in which a desire for freedom typical of youth finds expression—a freedom exercised by persons in community who are capable of encompassing diversity of race, social status, educational background. Diversity in community with respect for the individual person is then their goal.

All of the foregoing may appear superlative but unrealistic praise of the contemporary young adult and an extravagant condemnation of the older generation. It must be remembered that our subject here is "self-image"; space and indeed our purpose do not allow for an evaluation of that image or of the differences between it and what we chance to consider the reality. Let it suffice to say that contemporary young adults are restless and idealistic—and that much of what disquiets us today gives cause for hope, for it reflects not cynicism but disappointed idealism.

We who are teachers deal daily with the new community created by the young. We are confronted for perhaps the first time in history with young people as a whole generation denying absolutely not only the expectations of the earlier generation but the right of their elders to have such expectations. What do these young adults seek from us, what are they prepared to hear?

[6] *Ibid.*, p. 4.
[7] *Ibid.*, p. 1.
[8] Peter Schrag, quoted in Louis M. Savary, S.J., *The Kingdom of Downtown*, New York, Paulist Press, Deus Books, 1967, p. 30.

First of all, anyone who would make an impression on the now generation must be taught primarily to listen, and not merely to listen *to* but to listen *with*. In order to be heard by the contemporary young adult, the teacher of any discipline must begin where the student is—but he must know also where he, the teacher, is. He must be aware of the reciprocal relationship which is the *sine qua non* of effective dialogue in a student world from which the platform lecturer has vanished.

And then, for the theology teacher in particular, it is his painfully to discover that the "classical forms of symbolization and traditional patterns of belief" [9] are singularly irrelevant and meaningless to the young adult. If he goes by the "immutable ground rules by which the games of Catholic philosophy and theology are to be played," he will "function only within a certain clearly defined area of experience and preclude many of the most basic questions being asked today." [10] He faces, certainly, the collapse of the traditional language and discipline of theology when these are translated as the "technical generalizations and the ponderous formulations" [11] of his discipline. But conversely, he faces too the danger of yielding to an easy contemporaneity which disguises under the claim of relevance merely "a covert yearning for some simple rationalistic utopia, a fearful avoidance of the mysterious complexity of reality to which the lush tradition points." [12] To exchange the discipline of scholarship and the necessity of critical analysis for popular phrase-making is to betray the learning process.

The listening for God which the teacher of theology does with his students casts him, then, into the double role of poet and prophet. Neither poet nor prophet is easily accepted; neither can be concerned with personal comfort to the exclusion of his own charism. As poet and prophet, it is his role to open alternatives for young adults, to assure them by his living testimony that the important words—truth, love, faith and above all, hope—are realistic. As prophet, if not as poet, it is his to translate the Word of God into the here and now, to break into the world of man meaningfully, to permeate the lives of men with the content of that Word. This

[9] Walter H. Capps, "Contextualism in Religious Studies," paper delivered at the University of California at Santa Barbara, February 7, 1968, ms., p. 7.

[10] Monika Hellwig, "The Future of Theology," *Worldview*, February, 1968, p. 17.

[11] Myron B. Bloy, Jr., "Introduction," *The Church Review*, August, 1967, p. 1.

[12] *Ibid.*

means facing the emptiness of outmoded forms, rocking the boat, asking embarrassing questions about the status quo, challenging the Establishment. This means looking at lives which have been split by a modern schizoid mentality and endeavoring to heal them by the integration of God into life experience.

As poet, he will find or make new myths, analogues, out of film and folksong, out of dance and pop art, to inform the living of young adults with compassion, with faith, with fidelity in commitment. As poet, he will rediscover with Percy Bysshe Shelley a way of educating curiously ignored by the Christian tradition:

> The great secret of morals is love; or a going out of our nature, and an identification of ourselves with the beautiful which exists in thought, action, or person, not our own. A man, to be greatly good, must imagine intensely and comprehensively; he must put himself in the place of another and of many others; the pains and pleasures of his species must become his own. The great instrument of moral good is the imagination; and poetry administers to the effect by acting upon the cause.[13]

As poet and prophet, the theology teacher can celebrate and help others celebrate the "glad affirmation of God present within the facts of daily life" without "allowing those facts to intimidate" him or them.[14] For as prophet and poet, he knows that to celebrate truly is to exchange hilarity for humanity, and that to celebrate humanity is to "maintain" in the way the contemporary young adult uses that word today.

[13] "A Defense of Poetry," in Walter Jackson Bate, ed., *Criticism: the Major Texts*, New York, Harcourt, Brace and Company, 1952, p. 432.

[14] Harvey Cox, "Secularity," from the lecture series "Contemporary Dialogues on Growing Up in the Church," Culver City, California, March 31, 1968.

JOHN B. COBB, JR.

4 The Intrapsychic
Structure of Christian Existence

I

The problem of defining Christianity or of specifying what it means to be a Christian can be approached in several ways. It can be approached institutionally, with the understanding that a Christian is one who belongs to an institution which identifies itself as Christian. For statistical studies this is an appropriate method, but serious Christians know that institutional affiliation and genuine Christianity are not identical. It is obviously possible to be a church member for reasons that have little to do with Christianity.

A second approach is through belief. A Christian is understood as one who believes certain things, such as the divinity of Jesus, the authority of the church, or the doctrine of the Trinity. This approach also has its usefulness. Christians as a whole do believe some things that others do not generally believe. But two problems arise. First, diversity of belief among those sincerely identifying themselves as Christians is vast, and the specification of common beliefs is exceedingly difficult. Even when particular verbal formulas receive widespread acceptance, they carry very different meanings in different Christian groups. Second, most Christians do not regard cognitive assent to propositions as the essence of being Christian. Persons of impeccable orthodoxy in belief may still be regarded as not Christian. James's devils are a case in point.

A third approach is through ethics. A Christian is understood as one whose life conforms with certain ethical principles, who accepts responsibility for his society, or who is characterized by kindness in interpersonal relations. Here also two problems arise. First, much of Christian theology, especially in Protestantism, has sharply distinguished faith and works in such a way as to conflict with any definition of Christianity in ethical terms. The righteous pagan has not been regarded as a Christian. Second, those who are called Christian by such criteria may resent the claim. They understand themselves as Jews or humanists, Marxists or Buddhists, and see no justification for the Christian claim that their virtues are peculiarly Christian.

A fourth approach is to reject the attempt to distinguish Christians from others. To be a Christian, it is held, is simply to be a man, to be fully human. The sentence is not reversible. Hence the Christian makes no claim that only Christians can be fully human; the point is rather that as a Christian he is called to nothing else than full humanity. The problem with this approach is that it erroneously assumes that being fully human is a state which is easier to define than being Christian. To be fully human in a Buddhist context is something quite different from full humanity in a Christian context. The ideal of full humanity upheld by Freudian psychologists differs from that espoused by Jungians. It is certainly true that to be a Christian is to be fully human in the Christian sense. The question is, what is the distinctively Christian form of humanity?

To point out problems with these approaches is not to dismiss them. Any definition of Christianity which ignored its close relationship to the church, certain beliefs, and a particular ethic would be artificial. The fourth approach is commendable in its concern not to claim a monopoly for Christians on what Christians prize. It is preferable to define the norm and ideal without reference to institution and belief, recognizing that membership in the institution or orthodoxy in belief neither guarantees nor is essential to realization by individuals of the Christian goal. When this element of disconnection has been allowed for in the approach, then the question of positive relation can also be honestly raised and fully discussed. Perhaps after all the church and its beliefs *are* important for the realization of that humanity which is the Christian goal.

One term carefully avoided in the preceding discussion is *faith*. The presence of faith is the most common theological basis for denoting what it means to be a Christian. The problem here is that although almost all Christians would agree verbally to this criterion, there is no consensus on what is involved in faith. For some, faith refers to certain beliefs; for some, to trust; for others, to life affirmation. Faith can also mean actualization of a certain kind of humanity, namely, Christian humanity.

The distinctiveness of Christian humanity can best be considered when it is viewed as one mode of existence alongside others. Rudolf

Bultmann presents faith or Christian existence as authentic existence over against inauthentic existence. Both are understood in terms of Martin Heidegger's account of the structure of human existence. This is helpful, but the options are too limited. How are the modes of existence of Socrates and Gautama Buddha to be categorized in this scheme? They seem to be equally misrepresented whether they are classified as authentic or inauthentic.

Rather than attempt to categorize all the manifold modes of existence as either authentic or inauthentic in Heidegger's sense, it is better to develop a more flexible typology which allows for free expression of a variety of ideals as well as the corollary variety of ways in which men fail to achieve them. This means that there is a variety of structures of existence as well as a variety of modes of actualization of each structure.

In my book on *The Structure of Christian Existence,* I have tried to approach this question historically and with maximum flexibility of conceptuality. In the present essay, I can deal with it only schematically and in categories adapted chiefly to the Western scene.

To understand the diversity of structures, we can think of our existence in terms of five dimensions or levels: the body, the emotions, the reason, the will, and the spirit. This greatly simplifies the complex reality, neglecting, for example, such important aspects of our existence as our sensations, our imagination, and the creation and appreciation of beauty. Nevertheless, what is said about these dimensions will be enough to suggest how a more comprehensive account could be developed. It should be sufficient to allow us to avoid the oversimplifications introduced by those who stress only the unity of man as a psychophysical whole.

Each of these levels of our being has a certain independence of all the others and at the same time affects and is affected by all the others. A man's selfhood may be constituted at any one of these levels, and he may seek to become fully human from that perspective. For all men the body and the emotions are given, but the man who identifies himself with them may participate little or not at all in some of the other levels. Wholeness can thus be found most easily from a center in these foundational levels. Christian existence, on the other hand, involves the identification of the self with the spirit. The Christian quest for full humanity is the far more difficult quest for the excellence of all five dimensions unified around this center. Much of the following discussion will be devoted to explicating these briefly stated theses.

II

Discussion can best begin by considering the body and the emotions in their relation to each other. The body is easily defined as that which can be seen and touched and otherwise investigated by the physiologist. This includes, of course, the brain. Emotion, on the other hand, is much more difficult to define, especially since the word can be used to cover a variety of related phenomena. Hence I must try to make my own usage clear.

Every experience has both a subjective and an objective element. Something is presented to me in vision, in touch, in my awareness of events within my body, in my memory of past experiences, or conceptually. It is presented as a color, a texture, a pain, a moment of happiness, or a possibility that is not as such a mere part of the subjectivity of the subject. The color and texture are that of a sensory object; the pain is that of my leg or tooth; the happiness belonged to a past occasion; the possibility is an object of intellectual contemplation with a determinate relationship to other possibilities, given to me rather than caused by me. But this objective aspect of my experience is always accompanied by a subjective one. This subjective aspect is partly influenced by the objective and partly independent of it. A tone that in one moment is subjectively received as pleasant may in the next moment be boring and in a third maddening. When I remember a previous moment of happiness, there is a tendency for my present subjectivity to re-enact that happiness, but it need not do so. The subjective form of the memory may be melancholy. Even a pain, which seems more clearly than most sensations to impose its own form also on the subjective side of its psychic reception, can arouse also anger, fear, and even pleasure.

By *emotion* I mean this subjective side of the subjective-objective polarity that characterizes all experience. Emotion so understood has an exceedingly intimate relation to bodily functioning. It affects glandular secretions, the flow of blood, and visceral activity, for example. Some of these phenomena are so intimately associated with emotions that, when they occur for other reasons, the emotions themselves seem to occur. Also, a man's organic condition profoundly influences the subjective forms of the reception of numerous stimuli. Most of us are far more easily irritated when we are hungry or tired than when we are relaxed and well fed. To a considerable degree, our emotions can be influenced and even manipulated by drugs.

Despite the close interrelation between bodily functioning and emotions, they are not identical. This does not mean merely that they are defined in such a way as to indicate a difference, but also that neither is simply a function of the other. They are interdependent but also mutually independent.

This relation of *inter*dependence and *in*dependence is recognized in practice by most therapists. When a therapist is confronted by a physical disorder, he must consider that its cause may be purely physical. On the other hand, he must also recognize the possibility that its cause may be purely emotional. Similarly, an emotional symptom may have either a purely physical or a purely emotional cause. Usually both physical and emotional factors are involved in both physical and emotional symptoms, and if in origin the symptom resulted from only one, the presence of the symptom itself is likely to have had effects upon the other as well. Furthermore, even where the symptom and the cause are purely physical, emotions may assist or hinder the process of therapy; and even when the symptom and cause are purely emotional, good physical health can assist in recovery of emotional health.

In addition to stressing the intimate interdependence of bodily and emotional health, it is necessary to indicate how independent they can be. We all know persons of good physical health who have serious emotional problems, and we all know persons with serious physical handicaps and limitations who have nevertheless achieved a remarkable degree of emotional health. There is no full correlation of these two measures of health, and there are even occasions on which one must be sacrificed for the sake of the other. For example, one may have to lie still to allow a bone to heal even if that creates serious emotional problems.

The picture is greatly complicated when we introduce reason as another aspect of human existence. By *reason* I mean a kind of activity which presupposes an openness to the forms given in the objective pole of experience in some independence of their primary emotional impact. Once these forms are distanced in this sense, their mutual relations can be examined. This makes contemplation, analysis, classification, generalization, and speculation possible. It is these and related activities that are here classified as reason.

Reason is secondary in the sense that whereas physical and emotional levels of existence are essential, life and even human life can go on where reason is undeveloped. On the other hand, our world cannot survive without its intense cultivation. For *our* world is constituted largely of the cumulative achievements of reason in philosophy, science, technology, history, politics, and the arts.

The question now is that of the relation of health in this dimension of human existence to health in the bodily and emotional dimensions. While in recent times we have been taught to stress the *unity* of bodily and emotional life, we have learned to sense the *tensions* between healthy emotions and a major emphasis upon reason. Certainly in relation to body and emotion, reason is an independent variable. Few would assume a close correlation of bodily and emotional health on the one hand and rational excellence on the other; and the tensions between them are common and important.

To begin with an obvious example, the habit of critical distancing is in tension with the spontaneous emotions of romantic love. Even in less intimate relationships, a high development of rationality may stand in tension with the requisite natural warmth. The progressive rationalization of society in general disrupts communal ties and traditions that have had great emotional importance and value. That emotions, even healthy ones, can disrupt individual rational activity and prevent rational social reform is too obvious to require elaboration. The widespread enmity against reason in the name of the emotions is understandable.

Nevertheless, we should not understand the goals of emotional health and rational excellence primarily in their opposition. Emotional health must be defined in part in terms of the "reality principle," the capacity of individuals to accept and adjust to the reality known by reason. Reason can also be employed to understand emotional needs and to satisfy them. Indeed, a major agency of emotional healing is rational understanding of one's own emotions. On the other hand, reason is often prevented from carrying out its own activity by thwarted emotional needs, so that a certain degree of emotional health is prerequisite for clear thinking. We all know how many of the obstacles to learning are rooted in emotional grounds rather than in an inadequate capacity for reasoning.

Thus there is a relation both of interdependence and of independence between reason and emotion. In general, excellence of reasoning conduces to emotional health and vice versa. But we must also recognize that a high level of emotional health can occur where rational capacities are little developed and that rational excellence can exist along with an impoverished and distorted emotional life. Again, as with bodily and emotional welfare, one may even have to choose at times between rational and emotional health.

So far I have described relations of independence and interdependence characterizing the physical, emotional, and rational aspects of existence. In this discussion I expect general agreement since most of what has been said has a certain common-sense obviousness. There are theories, of course, which regard emotion as simply a function of physical events or reason as simply a function of emotion, but these theories violate our actual experience of ourselves and offer little guidance to those concerned with handling emotional and rational problems.

Where we introduce the *will*, however, the situation is quite different. The misleading character of this concept has often been stressed, and theoreticians have seriously tried to show how behavior, formerly attributed to it, is adequately understood as the resultant of other factors: it is quite possible to analyze the factors determinative of human behavior in terms of the interaction of emotion and reason. The rejection of the volitional as a distinctive dimension gains plausibility from the fact that we can rarely identify its workings with any clarity.

When we employ only the categories of emotion and reason to explain actions, we must assume that each of these forces operates according to its characteristic principles and that the resultant is determined by their respective strength. It is then meaningless to attribute "responsibility" for the outcome to the individual in question. However, most of us do so spontaneously, regarding both ourselves and others; we believe that the person in his unity is not to be seen in toto as the passive outcome of a struggle between emotion and reason. Instead we believe that, at least on some occasions, he can decide the outcome of this struggle from a perspective not identical to either reason or emotion, that is, by an "act of will."

That there is a distinctive activity properly designated in this way is attested by our sense of obligation and of sin. Furthermore, most of us can identify experiences in which we have come to a decision in a psychic act that is qualitatively different from thinking and feeling and in which the character of the decision reached is not experienced as dictated by the rational and emotional factors involved. That is, we can identify moments in our lives when reflection and emotional tension centering around uncertainty are resolved into definiteness of purpose, and in these moments it does not seem to be the emotions and thoughts alone that precipitate the resolution. Both the fact of the resolution and its form point to a third factor, the will. If in such relatively clear instances we can identify this factor, we can see it as functioning also, though less conspicuously or importantly, at other times.

The will is called into action by a problematic or decision situation. It can be described and identified without reference to specifically ethical considerations; but historically, the will emerged in situations where man was confronted continually by the either/or of obedience or disobedience, and it is doubtful that the will could have become a significant factor in the psyche apart from such a context. It is also doubtful that it can retain significance long after it loses such a context. The practical importance of the will is a corollary of an understanding of man as fundamentally an ethical being. The will then functions either in obedience or in disobedience to the ethical demand, and in this functioning it is free.

There does not exist as much parallelism between will on the one hand and emotion and reason on the other as between emotion and reason. The will has no inherent character comparable to that of emotion or reason. It exists as a transcendence of these factors—as the final determinant of behavior wherever the behavior is problematic. As long as the situation seems unambiguous, as long as there is no need to assume responsibility, the will remains negligible.

Where the will functions, however, it can have a massive effect upon the emotions and reason. One may will to cultivate certain emotions and to suppress others, and one may will to think a question through clearly or to close one's mind against disturbing facts. Also, the will can influence its own strength. One can will to cultivate the will, which means one can will not to allow one's behavior to be determined by the course of events but instead, again and again, to check one's spontaneous impulses and decide about them. Such a strengthening of the will in turn has consequences for the emotional and rational levels of existence.

The effect of the emotions and reason on the will, on the other hand, is more in terms of precondition than concrete determination. Apart from a certain level of emotional health, the will cannot emerge. An emotionally very sick person cannot be held responsible for conduct or, concomitantly, be understood as possessing a will. Also, even when the will is present, the range of conduct over which it can exert influence depends to a large extent on the health and development of emotional life. On the other hand, it is quite possible for emotional health to exist without any effective functioning of the will, and it is also possible for a rather strong development of will to occur where serious problems remain in the emotional life.

Similarly, there can be no functioning of the will apart from some development of rational powers. Also, the range of decisions available to the will is largely a function of reason and its resultant knowledge. Yet it is possible for rational reflection to reach great heights without the significant emergence of the will, and the will can achieve considerable strength in a man whose rational powers are limited. The correlation of emotional health and rationality on the one side and the development of the will on the other is positive, but far from total.

III

Another term, the *self*, is now needed to continue the discussion. By the *self* is here meant that center from which the totality of the psychic life is organized and unified. This center may be in the emotions. In that case, reason is felt as an instrument or weapon. Or the self may be located in reason, in which case the man perceives the emotional turmoil in his psyche as a strange and threatening force. Where the will occurs at all, it can do so only as a new center transcending emotion and reason—hence as a new locus of the self.

The question of the locus of the self is not identical to that of its strength. A man whose self is located in his reason or will, for example, may experience himself as overpowered by his emotions. Nevertheless, there is a close connection. The organization of the psychic life around emotions, reason, or will tends to strengthen that factor in relation to others.

The locus of the self in the emotions, reason, or will may be simply given. However, it is also possible for the self so to transcend itself that it freely determines its own locus. Where this occurs, there emerges an additional aspect of human existence which will be called *spirit*.

Of all the terms here used, *spirit* is the vaguest and most ambiguous. It is also the one most crucial to the exposition of Christian existence. The use of the term in this essay is most directly influenced by Reinhold Niebuhr and especially by *The Self and the Dramas of History*. But the explanation must be given independently.

Spirit is self-transcending selfhood. The notion of self-transcendence is used widely and with diverse meanings. It sometimes refers to man's capacity to view the present in the light of the past and the future. It sometimes means man's capacity provisionally to adopt perspectives other than his own. It sometimes suggests participation in a world of meanings in distinction from the world of facts. It can carry specifically religious overtones or point directly to man's experience of God.

Although these meanings are not alien to the present use, they are not definitive of it. Self-transcendence here refers primarily to an intrapsychic phenomenon. Since *self* has already been defined in these terms, it remains to define *transcendence,* so that the role of transcendence and of self-transcendence in the several modes of human existence can be distinguished and the uniqueness of spirit clarified.

Transcendence here means the capacity to distance or objectify and to act upon or to influence. All responsibility depends on transcendence in this sense. A man is responsible only for that which he can objectify and influence. On the other hand, transcendence does not insure responsibility, for responsibility in the full sense requires the sort of choosing which appears first with the will.

The self as will is transcendent over action, emotion, and reason. From the perspective of will, a man stands above his actions. He can allow his actions to be determined by his emotions, he can check them in terms of rational principles, or he can indulge in an arbitrary act of will. His will may be weak, in which case the effort of the self as will to control may fail, but even in this case it exists as a center which objectifies and acts upon other aspects of the psychic life.

Emotion and reason do not transcend will in this sense. When the center of a man's existence is in his emotional life or reason, there is no will. However, reason and emotion transcend each other in the sense that a self located in either is aware of the other as an alien force to be dealt with.

Furthermore, there are modes of self-transcendence to be found at each level. Even the self located in the emotions can have a kind of self-transcendence. Although there is a tendency for a man whose existence is so structured to be constantly changing according to his changing organic and environmental situation, the center of his being may become identical to certain emotions which he may thereby lift out of the flux of feeling and establish as enduring powerfully through many years. For example, the desire for revenge, aroused spontaneously in one situation, may become the permanent center of a man's existence in such a way that there is transcendence of the ordinary ebb and flow of emotional feeling. A man in whom this occurs may be called "strong-willed," but it is important to see that this is a different sense of "will" from that employed in this discussion.

Reason transcends itself in the fuller sense that the self which is centered in reason can think about the structure and principles of reason. The will, too, transcends itself in that a man may will to assert or to strengthen himself as will.

There is, however, a difference between the self's transcendence of itself qua reason or qua will and the self's transcendence of itself qua self. And although this may seem a subtle or merely verbal difference on initial consideration, it is in fact a profound one with vast consequences for human existence. It is a difference which comes clearly to expression in the work of Plato or the Pharisees on the one hand and Augustine on the other.

As will, a man is responsible directly for his actions and indirectly for the degree of his control of his actions. But he is not responsible for the locus of his self as will. His responsibility is directly proportional to his ability as will to determine action and is focused upon his action. The norm of health is the righteousness of this action.

The full reflexivity of self-transcendence that is spirit involves a new order of responsibility. As spirit, a man is responsible not only for his actions but more fundamentally for the locus of the self which acts. He is free as self to identify himself with emotion, reason, or will, and if he does so he is responsible for having adopted the form of selfhood which, if spirit were lacking, would be simply given. As long as he remains free to alter this self-identification, he remains spirit, but such self-identification may eventually destroy this possibility and hence destroy the spirit which initially effected it. The spirit retains its purity and full freedom as spirit only when it avoids this identification with other aspects of existence and instead identifies itself with itself as spirit, that is, with the power of radical self-transcendence.

Furthermore, man as spirit is responsible not only for the locus of his selfhood but also for its *character*. Whereas righteousness of will is a function of righteousness of conduct or of the intention to act rightly, excellence of spirit is a function of the *motivation* of conduct. Self-objectification of the self as self introduces possibilities for destructive preoccupation with self which are absent to the self which is constituted as emotion, reason, or will. It introduces also the ideal possibility of a new kind of love for the other, which is independent of the attractiveness of the other.

Responsibility depends upon transcendence combined with the power of choice. These conditions are realized as fully at the level of spirit as at the level of will. But whereas at the level of will such transcendence and choosing can be quite simply equated with the power to act, at the level of spirit this is not true. A self constituted as will is not responsible to act in a way in which he cannot act, but a self constituted as spirit is responsible for unloving motivation far beyond the point of any simple ability to change that motivation. The Kantian view that obligation implies ability applies at the level of will, but more paradoxical formulations are required to explain the experience of the spiritual man.

The relation of spiritual excellence to the well-being of other aspects of existence is formally parallel to the relations considered above. This means that, on the whole, emotional health, developed rationality, and a well-established will tend to further spiritual life, but they do not guarantee even the presence of spirit, much less its rich fulfillment. Similarly, a high quality of spiritual life tends to promote emotional health, rationality, and the volitional side of existence, but it is no guarantee of freedom from weakness in these other areas.

For example, whereas emotional neurosis handicaps the total psychic development and inhibits the excellence of the spirit, man may spiritually overcome such a handicap. An emotionally sick person may yet be a saint! This means also that the spiritual transcendence of such handicaps need not involve overcoming the neurosis itself. On the other hand, such a spiritual achievement does constitute a context in which the chances of emotional healing are enhanced.

The relation of spirit to reason is similar but not identical. Whereas emotional life is part of all human existence, reason is a special dimension of existence not uniformly effective among all men. Reason can be highly developed without the presence of spirit, and spirit can be present where many of the higher forms of reason are undeveloped. On the other hand, a certain measure of rationality is essential to the occurrence of spirit, and the presence of spiritual health can facilitate genuine rationality by freeing a man to be more and more formed in his understanding by the objective situation and to distort his judgments less and less in terms of self-interest and self-justification.

The most intimate relation is that between spirit and will. Since spirit arises as a transcendence of will, it cannot exist where the will is not present. However, the emergence of the spirit alters the character of the will. What had been the self becomes an instrument or agency of the self.

In considering the body and the emotions, the distinction between the strength and the health of these aspects of human existence was not elaborated. The distinction would have been discussed more thoroughly had space allowed. With respect to will and spirit and the correlation between them, this distinction is essential.

Strength of will is the degree to which the will dominates emotion and reason in the control of action. Health of will is the righteousness of the action it intends. Strength of spirit is the degree to which spirit maintains itself in its transcendence of the other aspects of existence and succeeds in subordinating the whole psychic life to itself. Health of spirit is genuine concern for others as opposed to preoccupation with the self.

A man of strong will may exercise his will either righteously or unrighteously. The same is true of a man of weak will. Likewise, a man of strong spirit may be either spiritually sick or spiritually healthy—either self-preoccupied or genuinely concerned for others and their needs. And the same is true of a man of weakly developed spirit. On the other hand, there is no complete neutrality here. Repeated disobedience tends to weaken the will, and self-preoccupation tends to weaken the spirit.

Strength of spirit usually presupposes strength of will; yet it is possible for a man of relatively weak will to have a fully developed spiritual transcendence. Certainly spiritual strength is possible for a man who exercises his will unrighteously. It even seems possible for a man who is often unrighteous in the exercise of his will to be relatively healthy spiritually, and certainly a very righteous man may be spiritually very sick. Thus, in all of these relations, we find again the pattern of mutual interdependence combined with a measure of independence.

IV

Spiritual existence is the structure of Christian existence. It can be either healthy or unhealthy. *Christian existence is healthy spiritual existence*, that is, spiritual existence which expresses itself in Christian love.

If love is defined broadly, no man lacks it wholly. No one is so depraved as to be totally devoid of fondness or tenderness toward some other person. But such fondness or tenderness does not by itself qualify as Christian love. Christian love is not emotional attraction, ecstatic loss of self, or the desire to possess. It is rather the genuine concern of a self-transcending self for another person, independent of any emotional reaction to him—a concern which seeks the other's freedom also from the lover. It has an emotional element, which often includes fondness and tenderness, but this accompanies the concern as its product rather than determining its object.

Most of us who share in the heritage of Christian civilization participate to some degree in Christian love. But few would dare to claim that their relations to any other person are entirely characterized by this kind of love. Our total motivation in all our relationships involves such elements as self-seeking, a wish for approval, emotional liking and disliking, and the desire to be righteous. Alongside such elements there may or may not be Christian love. When it is present at all, it may be one factor among others, influencing but not determining the action, or it may in certain moments be decisive and overrule other elements present in the total motivation.

The extent to which Christian love can influence our total relation to another person depends partly upon its strength within the structure of spiritual existence and partly upon the strength of that structure. Although the strength of spiritual existence does not determine the presence or absence of Christian existence, Christian existence when present is strong or weak according to the strength of the spirit. What is definitive of Christian existence is the health of spiritual existence. But the Christian must be almost as much concerned about the strength of the spirit, apart from which Christian love inevitably proves ineffectual. Here, too, we are dealing with a matter of degree.

A man may accept responsibility for himself in a total, wholehearted way, becoming increasingly aware of all that this entails, or he may do so hesitantly and reluctantly, remaining blind to much in that self for which he accepts tentative responsibility. Similarly, a man may habitually objectify or transcend himself, or he may do so occasionally and only fleetingly. Finally, although spirit exists only as the self or seat of existence, the capacity of the self to control other aspects of psychic life effectively varies greatly. A man may as spirit clearly determine the direction of his experience and action, or he may find his spiritual selfhood overwhelmed by other psychic forces. Strength of spirit varies in all these ways, and in doing so it determines also the quality of participation in Christian existence.

Finally, although the *distinctive* concern of Christian existence is strong and healthy spiritual existence, the Christian ideal is for strength and health at every level of existence. Strength and health of spirit do not guarantee strength and health of body, emotion, reason, or will; and as noted above, the pursuit of strength or health at one level requires a man at times to pay a price at other levels. But the Christian goal remains the strength and health of the whole man centering around a strong and healthy spirit. Clearly, approximation to this goal can take many forms.

In all these respects, participation in Christian existence is a matter of degree. In a world where direct Christian influence becomes ever more pervasive through the widespread process of Westernization, it may be that some element of such participation is now almost universal. Nevertheless, there is nothing about the human situation as such which guarantees to any man participation in Christian existence. On the contrary, through most of the millennia of history over most of the globe, human existence has lacked the kind of self-transcendence which is spirit. Even in its heartland, for many men participation in spiritual existence has been weak and sporadic; and now, just as the Westernization of the world promises the widest spread of spiritual existence, new ideals and new modes of existence are appearing in the West in which spirit is simply absent. Even where spirit is present and affirmed, and with it the structural conditions for Christian love, that love may be absent. Thus not only in the past but also in the present and future, participation both in the spiritual structure of existence and in its Christian form is not simply a matter of degree but also a matter of either/or. Christian existence constitutes one mode of existence, one possibility, one ideal, among others.

V

Christian existence has been defined without reference to particular beliefs, modes of conduct, or institutions, and it is clear that participation in Christian existence is not always closely correlated with explicit Christianity as judged by these measures. At the same time, Christian existence has been defined as a mode of existence which is historically conditioned and by no means necessitated by universal elements in the human situation. Hence the question arises of how Christian existence emerged in history and how it has been sustained. Still more important is the question of what is now required if Christian existence is to survive the present period of confusion. It is clear that in the past certain beliefs, practices, and institutions have been closely associated with Christian existence, and yet that much of the spread of Christian existence has been only indirectly dependent upon them. One who is committed to the preservation and strengthening of Christian existence must attempt to identify those features of traditional Christianity which seem to be essential to calling future generations into Christian existence. There would still remain, of course, the question of whether those features of the tradition can be carried forward today with integrity.

Appropriate discussion of these questions would require a second paper, but a brief statement of my views will serve to point the direction in which further reflection is needed. It is my opinion that in the long run Christian existence cannot flourish apart from belief in and worship of God as he is known in Jesus. The following points, while far from proof or even justification of this opinion, may indicate the kinds of considerations which I find persuasive.

First, men do not accept radical responsibility for what they are except as they are confronted with a call to be something that they are not and cannot easily become. If we are asked to do what we can easily do, we are quickly satisfied with ourselves. If we are confronted with an ideal in such a way that we find ourselves responsible for failing to realize it, the possibility of spiritual existence is present. Such a confrontation we experience in relation to God as we know him in Jesus.

Second, men will not be concerned fundamentally for the motives of their own actions if these motives have no reality for anyone except themselves. Our interest in ourselves is ultimately a function of the interest we have in how we appear to others. Apart from belief in the biblical God, who looks upon the heart, major aspects of our inner life will lose their importance for us. Christian existence is impossible where there is no acceptance of radical responsibility for motives as well as acts.

Third, men will not prize spiritual life, and hence will not sustain it indefinitely, when it constitutes itself as self-preoccupation. But self-preoccupation can be overcome at the level of spiritual existence only by a self-acceptance, which is a function of acceptance by others. Only an ultimate forgiveness can constitute adequate acceptance, and only the God who is known in Jesus can be the subject of such a forgiveness.

Finally, the experienced reality of the God whom we know in

Jesus is mediated as much through participation in worship as through instruction and discussion. The worship may be private, but few can indefinitely sustain such devotion without the discipline and support of a community. Apart from a worshiping community, the prospects for Christian existence are dark.

T. PATRICK BURKE

5 Evidence and Convictions

At the present time, I think it is true to say, a large number of Catholics are going through a crisis of faith. That is not a new thing among Protestants; perhaps it is not at all a bad thing for Christianity to be facing even an internal crisis. But it is both new and desperately painful to this generation of Catholics. They were brought up to believe that there was no room for questioning in matters of faith. Now they find many things questioned, even by leaders of their religious community. Numbers of Catholics feel they are approaching the edge of an abyss: where is the questioning going to stop?

This crisis is concerned with particular *convictions*. Did Jesus rise from the dead? Was Jesus God? Is God personal? Is there a God at all? And of course, as a result, has Christianity any absolute value? It has become a matter of great urgency to find at least some viable *method* of arriving at an answer to these questions (although, strangely, that particular fact is not yet widely recognized, I think, in the Catholic community). Whether we answer yes or no, and even if we say it doesn't matter, we must still give an account of why we answer the question the way we do. We must have some reason for believing what we believe. Any attempt to build religion on blind faith in the long run destroys religion and faith. It appears to me no coincidence that the theology of Karl Barth has led to atheistic theology. And the present trend in Catholic thinking along the same line, as shown for example in Cirne-Lima's statement that faith is unreasonable, can only end at the same result.

Taking the term *reason* in its broadest sense, our final court of appeal is our own reason. To say this is to say that we must have some sort of evidence for our religious convictions. That is the question to which this chapter is devoted. What sort of thing would constitute evidence for a religious conviction? To speak in terms of images of man, we are concerned not only with man the irrational, with the subconscious, the emotional, and the absurd, but with man trying to be rational (admitting that religion is a curious mixture of all of these).

Now I am going to put the matter of religion aside for the moment, and ask the question in more general terms. For this purpose, I am going to consider a number of propositions taken from other fields, and in each case ask the question, what sort of thing would constitute evidence for the proposition?

1. *The number −1 has a square root.*

Logically, the proposition appears self-contradictory. If you multiply two minuses together, you always get a positive number. No one has ever seen the square root of −1; it seems in its own nature to be impossible. And yet it is a commonplace in mathematics. What sort of thing would constitute mathematical evidence for the proposition? One mathematician expressed it recently by saying that it depends entirely on your point of view.[1] If you look on the square root of −1 as a simple number, then it is logically impossible. But you can also look on it as what is called a complex number, or operator, in which case the difficulty disappears. It would take too long here to go into the reasons for this; they can be found in any math textbook. The point is that even in a science like mathematics, what constitutes evidence can depend on the point of view you adopt, on the way you look at things.

2. *There is an unlimited number of subatomic particles.*

It is obvious that such a proposition could never be experimentally verified in itself. It is only possible to carry out a limited number of experiments, and so it is only possible to discover a limited number of particles by direct experiment, even granting that an electron was capable of being observed. But there is one way in which the proposition can be verified experimentally: by proving a larger theory which includes it. Yet once the larger theory is verified, the question nonetheless arises, how necessary is this particular proposition really to the theory as a whole? In point of fact, I think it is

---

[1] W. W. Sawyer, *Mathematician's Delight,* Harmondsworth, Eng., Penguin Books, Pelican series, 1968.

true to say that much of what is accepted in contemporary physics is accepted on that basis.

3. *At the beginning of the Middle Ages, Europe was an open society. By the middle of the fourteenth century, it had become a closed society.*

What sort of thing would constitute evidence for this proposition? Again, it obviously cannot be verified by experiment—we cannot put the Middle Ages in a test tube. Does that invalidate the proposition or render it meaningless? No; we decide to give a certain meaning to the phrase "open society," and then we examine records which have the appearance of coming from that period. Let us say we are dependent almost entirely on written documents describing a certain state of affairs, for example, the *Chronica regia coloniensis,* which gives a horrible picture of the activities of the German inquisitor Conrad of Marburg in the 1230s. We have to ascertain not only whether the document really dates from that time but also whether it is worthy of belief. Perhaps there are other reports which give us a contrary picture, from Conrad's side. How are we going to decide which one to believe? Ultimately, in judging the credibility of any historical document, we are thrown back on such judgments as whether it is consistent with itself and whether it is tendentious or biased.

And yet no one document could suffice as evidence for such a general assertion as is contained in proposition 3. What would constitute evidence for it, then, would be a *multitude* of reliable descriptions dating from that time and all pointing in the same direction. That is, a judgment could be made on the basis of a sufficient number of individual indications no one of which would ever be enough by itself. What would constitute a sufficient number? To answer this question, we would have to weigh and balance the strength of this indication against the force of that one, until we considered that the combination of indications was strong enough.

4. *Almost all human behavior is predetermined by subconscious forces.*

Here we have a different situation. In this case, it is not so much a matter of ascertaining observable facts; the visible phenomena of human behavior are familiar to us. No doubt some psychological experiments conducted on animals show an interesting parallel with human reactions. And no doubt the use of various forms of therapy can provide information on the grounds for certain patterns of behavior. But in the end, there is no way the proposition can be verified by experimentation. Yet there are many people in the field of psychology who accept it. What sort of thing would constitute evidence for it?

The observable facts remain the same. What is at issue is the *explanation* of the facts. Various interpretations of the visible manifestations are possible. The question then occurs, which interpretation explains them more adequately—that is, with the fewest postulates while accounting for all the phenomena? If I accept the theory, it is not because I have discovered some new facts but because this theory has the appearance of fitting the facts I already know better than another.

The situation is similar to Copernicus'. The data he possessed were the same as his predecessors had possessed. In theory, the explanations given by either Ptolemy or Copernicus could account for all the data. But it was seen that Copernicus' interpretation was more satisfactory because it was simpler.

On what basis would we adopt or discard the theories of a Freud, an Adler, or a Jung? The results obtained by these approaches are almost identical: in each case, some 30 percent of the patients are cured, I am told. Our basis would be that we considered one account a more adequate or more satisfying explanation of life as we experience it than another.

5. *Harold Pinter's play,* The Caretaker *is a fine drama.*

On what sort of evidence could we make that judgment? It would be possible on emotional grounds: I have seen the play; I have become caught up in it, puzzled by the banality of the dialogue, yet curiously sympathetic with the absurdity of the characters, and gripped by the tension of waiting for the unexpected. But my judgment is not simply a statement about my own reactions to it; I am capable of criticizing my own emotional responses to a play. My judgment on the play is precisely about it, not me. I say that it is a good work of art.

Implicit in my emotional reaction is the opinion that in some way the play penetratingly represents a dimension of real life. I have had a certain experience of life, an experience which contains many dimensions and levels. And when I see this play, I say to myself: that is what life is really like. Not that all the people I meet are mentally defective as are the characters in the play; it does not correspond literally with the surface of life. But it portrays a dimension of life which I recognize as soon as I see it acted out.

6. *A proposition which is not a tautology has meaning only if some sense experience is relevant to its verification.*

This is a form of the famed verification principle of logical positivism. What sort of thing would be evidence for it? It has been pointed out often enough that it unfortunately does not verify itself. Some are apparently content to call it a convention. But if it is merely a convention, then we are justified in asking, why adopt this one rather than another? If it is a convention, it can be one only in the way in which, say, Ockham's Razor is a convention, that is, one which the nature of our mind requires us to accept. There is no real reason that an explanation with fewer postulates should be more accurate than one with more. But if we worked on any other principle, if we just multiplied postulates at will, reasoned life would become impossible.

Likewise, there is something which could constitute evidence in support of the verification principle: if it should turn out, for example, that it makes sense, in such a way that not to adhere to it would make intellectual life impossible in practice.

But is it really such a line of reasoning which has led the logical positivists to adopt the principle? Analytic philosophy has been defended with all the intolerance of a religious faith. What is it, in actual fact, that leads a person to become a logical positivist rather than an existentialist or a metaphysician? Is it not his particular experience of life, and his persuasion that the total viewpoint represented by this philosophy seems to him to correspond most realistically with that experience? What is at stake is not the principle of verification as such but a whole approach to life. This is why the principle itself could undergo such alterations as it has, while the basic commitment of so many to it has remained.

7. *"I cannot refuse to hope: for me to despair would be to deny all the love that has been shown me."*

The sentence is taken from an essay on "Why Do I Hope?" by the former United States ambassador to Russia, George F. Kennan.[2] Is there any sort of thing which would constitute evidence that to

[2] George F. Kennan, *Why Do I Hope?*, Princeton, Princeton University Press, 1966.

despair would be to deny the love that has been given to me? The relationship cannot be proved by logic or analysis: the notion of denying love is not contained implicitly in the notion of despair. Is the statement simply an emotional one? Clearly it has strong emotional overtones. But the assertion cannot be categorized simply as emotion or reason. It is larger than that. It concerns a way of looking at life, a manner of understanding reality. And the only thing that could be evidence for it is my experience of life, that is, my experience of love, despair, and hope. In the light of my experience of these things, an experience which includes some idea of their implications, I look at the statement and I say either yes, that makes sense, or no, it does not make sense.

By now it is probably evident what I am going to say about the sort of thing which I think constitutes evidence for religious convictions.

In the first place, I would like to suggest that *experience* is something broader than we frequently imagine it to be. In addition to sense-based observation, there is the mental or intellectual experience of *seeing* that an idea or a viewpoint *makes sense* because it fits in better with life as we have lived it, the perception that a certain explanation corresponds with the facts more adequately than another. Perhaps we could call this noetic experience. It was this sort of experience which was evidence in propositions 2, 4, 5, 6, and 7.

When I say that the explanation "fits in" or "corresponds" with life better, I do not mean psychologically—for example, that it fills a need which we feel. It is no guarantee of Christianity's truth, for example, that it provides us with consolation; in those terms, it might simply be escapism from the harsher realities of life. I mean that it makes sense as an explanation, intellectually. However, this does not make it a matter of logic. There is no process of logical reasoning by which we could deduce that our experience of life is better accounted for in one way than in another. It can only be a question of *seeing* what fits, as when doing a jigsaw or crossword puzzle. We look at life, and we look at various views of life, and we *see* that one view is more adequate than others.

Of course, we can misinterpret both life itself and the various ways of understanding it which we encounter. We can fail to give proper consideration to large and important dimensions of life by concentrating on one or another aspect of it. And we can fail to do justice to one explanation by simply taking another for granted. If we are to act intelligently, then we need to *look* long, carefully, and comprehensively at our experience of life on the one hand and, on the other, at the ways of understanding it which present themselves to us.

In the second place, it will be clear that what is at stake is the evidence for the Christian view of things *as a whole*, not primarily for a particular conviction. Does the Christian faith *as a totality* fit in more adequately with our experience of life than other and competing explanations? If it does, that constitutes the evidence for it. No religious conviction exists in isolation. It is always held as part of a totality. In this respect, the same thing is true of religion as of *King Lear* or Jackson Pollock's painting *Number One* or the quantum theory. If I simply take one portion of it—for example, one segment of the painting—it may make no sense at all by itself. What makes sense is the totality, and that in terms of our experience of life.

With regard to a particular issue, then, such as Jesus' resurrection, the question becomes: to what extent is the idea of Jesus' resurrection a necessary part of Christianity? That is a different question, a most important one which belongs ultimately in the domain of hermeneutics, but it has to be judged by different criteria.

A further comment also seems needed. I do not intend this notion of evidence in a purely subjective sense. No doubt there are great differences in the experience people have of life, and it is very likely that a person will be strongly influenced by his own temperament and circumstances. But there is also a certain experience of life which is common to all men, and it is my contention that this is the test we have to apply. Evidence is something which is not simply private and personal. What makes sense can be articulated in such a way that a number of people can agree on it, and one person can convince another that it is valid. The question is, then, is this particular religious system, taken as a whole, a more adequate interpretation than others of mankind's *general* experience of life?

Finally, I should observe that religious or theological convictions as such are statements not about things in themselves but about their *meaning* for us. Religion and hence theology are concerned with any topic of inquiry only insofar as it has significance for man and his salvation. Of course, the whole point of any religion is that the salvation of man is to be found in a God or gods. Precisely because

religion is concerned with man's salvation, it is centered on God—
thus is Christianity centered on Jesus—but from the point of view
that God (and here, Jesus) is our salvation.

Religious convictions about Jesus, for example, are primarily convictions about the manner in which man is *saved*, not whether
Jesus was or was not God or did or did not rise from the dead. It
is only this religious conviction, concerning significance or meaning,
which can be binding on a religious community. Once the question of Jesus' salvific import for man has been settled, the way is
open for various philosophical and historical conceptions of Jesus,
such as we find in the course of Christianity—what is to be understood by the hypostatic union, for example, or by Jesus' resurrection
from the dead. The same is true of the idea of God: once a group
has agreed on the significance that God has for man, this leaves room
for a number of metaphysical conceptions of what God is like—
Augustine's idea of him as *ipsum esse,* Pseudo-Dionysius' conception
of God as beyond all being, or Tillich's Ground of Being. All of
these notions are legitimate, but none can be religiously binding
because they are philosophical, not religious, statements.

The present crisis of faith cannot be dealt with simply by saying
that faith is a personal relationship, essential though that is, because
the crisis concerns *conviction.* (How can I have a personal relationship with God if God is not personal?) That is to say, we must
discover some *method* of deciding what convictions we are going
to hold as Christians and what we are not going to hold (what are
reasonable and what unreasonable).

On the other hand, it is widely assumed in the empiricist world
in which we live that religious convictions are incapable of verification, or in other words, that there is no experience which could
count as evidence either for or against them.

What I have tried to do is suggest that there is a form of evidence
which can be applied to religious convictions, and that it lies in our
seeing that the total picture presented by a religious view *makes
sense* in terms of our experience of life. This I have called, for lack
of a better name, noetic experience.

I am now faced with the question: what sort of thing would
constitute evidence that my thesis about the evidence for religious
convictions is true? This seems a good place to stop, especially since
I discover to my surprise that it is the last question I have asked
myself.

JOHN A. HUTCHISON

6 Humanism and the World's Faiths

I have a visual representation—Plato might call it a myth, or the Bible might speak of a parable—which will make clear the main contentions of this discussion. Imagine if you will a circle with a crowd of people around the circumference and at the center a somewhat puzzled little man who keeps repeating, "Who am I? Why am I here?" The people around the circumference appear to be calling to the man in the middle, seeking to answer his questions. They are saying many different things and are speaking in many different languages, some of them comprehensible to the observer and some of them incomprehensible. Some of their assertions conflict with each other; others seem to agree. Some of the people around the circumference quarrel with each other, others agree, and still others seem oblivious to the presence of anyone else. At times these people seem unpleasant and discourteous to the man in the middle. Among their varied answers the man in the middle must choose, and in terms of his choice must live out his life. Such, I shall argue, is the contemporary relation of the faiths of the world to each other and to man or humankind, to whom presumably these faiths are addressed.

In explication of this parable, I shall have something to say first about the contemporary situation of man, second about the explanation of the man in the middle by means of the philosophy called existentialism, third about the first word in the title of this chapter —humanism, and fourth about the world's faiths as symbols, systems which aim or seek to answer the human question.

Concerning the contemporary situation, it is one in which faith is a matter of free choice and decision in a sense radically new in

human history. In other words, whatever faith a man is to hold and
live by, he must achieve it by his own choice and hold it in freedom.
This situation is first of all a consequence of modern and contemporary history. Men and peoples are meeting and mingling today
as never before in history. As a result, more than one option of faith
presents itself for a man's appraisal. Therefore, faith inevitably becomes a matter of choice or decision.

Another factor in modern history converges upon this same result. Throughout the modern period, initially in the West but increasingly throughout the world, a criticism of tradition has operated
—in religion, in morals, in politics, and I think in every other aspect
of human culture. Indeed, it is not far wrong to define modernity in
terms of the criticism of tradition. In the case of religious tradition,
this has led many people of unquestioned intelligence and good will
to a more or less complete rejection of all traditional religious forms
—forms of belief, forms of practice, and forms of feeling. Now,
whether any one of us as an individual goes along with this attitude
is not the point; whatever one's individual attitude, the impact of
this modern posture has made all faith a matter of conscious choice
or decision. No longer is it possible to grow into a tradition and to
live in it as a fact of social status or natural landscape.

That faith is a matter of free decision accords well with the principles of the many religions which have placed choice or decision at
the heart of the human situation. These faiths say to man, "Choose
whom or what you will serve," though it is of course a fact that
religious practice has often lagged far behind principle in this as
in other respects. However, there are also in the wide world other
traditional religions in which faith has been conceived as a matter
not so much of individual choice as of social participation and status.
Shinto is one such; another is popular Hinduism. It is a large and as
yet unanswered question whether these religions will be able to respond successfully to the new environment.

Freedom of religious decision, then, seems to be man's fate in the
contemporary world. Yet I propose that we make a virtue of this
necessity. Many of the traditional faiths have a profound understanding of the freedom of the human spirit; many of them have held
the theory that faith must properly be achieved and held in freedom.
Let us grasp the nettle of freedom. Let us say plainly that only a
faith which is achieved and maintained in full freedom and responsibility has any human validity or authenticity. Let the people standing around the circumference of the circle in our parable plainly

instruct the man in the middle concerning his free nature, encouraging him to think and decide freely and to hold whatever faith he may choose in his full human stature of freedom and responsibility. Such a proposal draws out and makes explicit the freedom which is at least implicit in many of the world's religious traditions.

This notion of free choice requires at least one important qualification. It is that man's finite nature must always limit his freedom. Human finitude implies partiality in both senses of this word, namely, incompleteness and partisanship. One implication of finitude may be stated in terms of the range of freedom of choice. To assert that the little man in the middle of our circle is able to look all around the circumference and then in some impartial, Olympian way make his choice is to impute to him an omniscience which no finite, mortal creature ever possessed. For any existing man or group of men, large sections of the circle are blocked out by partiality of outlook. Any man's occupancy of an altogether particular part of time and place effectively limits his vision, and often skews it as well.

If I may put this point autobiographically, I would have to say that despite considerable interest of many sorts, I have never had any real motivation to convert to Buddhism or Hinduism. Hence I must conclude that my own range of choice is limited accordingly. To cite another kind of illustration, I have for many years taught courses in the religions of mankind; and I have learned that to expound any faith effectively, I must empathize with it. The teacher must imagine what it feels like to be an adherent of the faith he seeks to teach. But to do this genuinely and effectively is not easy, and I know how imperfect one's best efforts are. Incidentally, these limits constitute no excuse for not doing the best one can to exercise and stimulate in others the highest degree of freedom of which human nature is capable.

In the second place, we may come to a better understanding of the man in the middle of the circle in our parable by means of a brief exposition of the movement called existentialism, which has now been with us long enough for us to begin to understand it and put it to work for us. Existentialism may be roughly characterized as an intellectual movement which began in the nineteenth century (though with roots going back to earlier periods) and came to flower in the twentieth, and which embraces philosophy, theology, and literature and other arts. The movement centers in the question, "What is man?" or perhaps more personally and poignantly, "Who am I?" The question is pressed with great passion, and is often asked in the midst of an agonizing sense of alienation or estrangement from true selfhood. Sometimes it takes the form, "Prior to all rational theories, what am I *really* or *actually?*" At other times it is worded, "Beyond all alienation, who or what am I *authentically?*" In any case, we note that the existence referred to in existentialism is the existence of man, of *me* or of *us*. We also note more than incidentally that the defining question of existentialism is precisely the question put by the man in the middle in our parable.

It is important to note that the existentialist question has defining force. Man *is* the creature who asks this question, the being in whom, in other words, the life impulse becomes self-conscious long enough to voice such questions as "Who am I? Whence? Whither? Why?" Stated another way, in man *existence* precedes *essence*. *That* man is, that he exists, takes precedence over *what* he is or may become. This observation is obviously not true of objects like chairs or typewriters, in whose being essence and existence are bound together in inextricable union where there is no shadow of separation between *that* and *what*. Similarly, there is no observable cleavage between essence and existence in animal nature. For example, the dog does not appear to have any problems about his caninity. If our family dog asks herself, "What must I do and be to be genuinely canine?" she keeps it a deep secret from the human members of the family. Likewise, the cow in her pasture seems unconcerned with problems of her bovinity; she gives no evidence of asking, "How can I achieve genuine bovinity?"

In sharpest possible contrast, man's essence, namely, his humanity (however we may define his humanity), is a problem to him. At the heart of every serious human personality lies the question, "What must I do and be to be genuinely human?" It is formulated in many and various ways, but in some form or other it may be characterized as *the* human question. It is moreover a question which men answer not in a classroom or study and not even at pleasant dinner meetings, but in deed and life. Man's real answer to this question is the answer which he lives out—the answer which finds articulation in his active life.

Existentialism has focused attention not only upon the question, "What is man?" but also upon the value or values which are asserted as working answers to this question. These values vary widely. Nietzsche's answer differs from that of Kierkegaard or Dostoevski. Sartre's answer differs from Buber's. However, in all this diversity one value upon which all existentialists seem to agree is man's fundamental freedom. Whatever answers a man gives to the questions, "Who am I?" and "Why am I alive?" he must give them freely if they are to have any validity. In freedom and responsibility he must live out his answer. This means that each human self is, as Whitehead once remarked, a bid for freedom. And through freedom it is a bid for human fulfillment or realization.

The word *humanization* has been popularized of late by Teilhard de Chardin as a designation for the lifelong process by which a man achieves and sustains his humanity. Perhaps not quite incidentally, the negative term *dehumanization* is older and better known. Together these two polar words define a struggle which goes through the heart of every man and yet which extends out to the whole human race. Each human life is a battleground for this fight; but so also is that larger event of history called humanity!

The existential question has both a timeless and a timely character. In other words, wherever and whenever in this world or any other world there are human beings, the existential question or something like it will be close to the center of their individual and their common lives. Yet it is also true to say that the issues of modern and contemporary history have pushed this question to the center of our concern, and have given it a consciousness and an intensity which it lacked in other times and places. In terms of our parable, the man in the middle is everyman. He speaks for all of us as men. Yet in a peculiar sense, he speaks for contemporary man, for man in our troubled and tumultuous twentieth century.

I come now in the third place to the important and multivalued word *humanism*. Our task here is to sort out and arrange among its many meanings those which bear importantly on the predicament of the man in the middle of our circle. In the ancient Greco-Roman world, humanism found expression in Protagoras' teaching that man is the measure of all things, or in Horace's resolution to hold nothing human alien to him. Through the centuries of the Western world, humanism in its most basic sense has continued to be the assumption of a human measure or standard of excellence and fulfillment which draws within its synoptic vision many wide and varied forms of experience. The life of individual human beings is thought to be broadened, deepened, and elevated—in short, humanized—by relation to this humanistic ideal. This achievement—or better, this initiation—is thought to take place by way of the lifelong development of one's human potentialities through education in the arts and sciences.

The humanistic ideal has shown a continuing capacity for growth and transformation throughout Western history. During the Middle Ages, a religious dimension was added. Was not man made in the image of God for the high destiny of fellowship with his maker? The Renaissance in its turn protested against some of the extremes and excesses of the religious spirit, asserting an inherent dignity and value in man's present experience. Not God but man is the valid center of our human concerns, said the Renaissance. The Enlightenment broadened and deepened this same theme, adding the new and powerful element of natural science with its strong emphasis on rationalism and the ethic of humanitarianism. This, or something like this, is in briefest, barest outline the classical Western ideal of humanism.

Sometime during the early nineteenth century, a new and different meaning was given to the word *humanism*. The word *God* had become increasingly distasteful in high intellectual society, and the term *Man* (with a capital *M*) was substituted. We cannot and need not here chronicle this development from Hume and Voltaire through Comte and Feuerbach and Thomas Huxley to John Dewey, Corliss Lamont, and the American Humanist Association. Suffice it to say that in this new meaning, the term *humanist* became a label for men who, unable to believe in God, resolved still to believe in Man. Despite many continuities in valuation with traditional humanism (and traditional Christianity), the new meaning has tended to emphasize the discontinuity from tradition.

I bring up these various uses and changing developments because I want to propose here still a newer and different meaning for the term. Indeed, it might be argued that it is not I who propose this change but rather contemporary history, which is placing a new global context around the word; I seek simply to report the new development. In this change, incidentally, it is not necessary to deny the term *humanism* to John Dewey, Julian Huxley, and their followers in the humanist associations of America and Europe, but only to challenge their exclusive right to the word. What I wish to propose is that there are in the world today many value systems which may and do compete for the use of the term *humanism*, and no one of which has exclusive rights. The argument of this paper is in effect to legitimize this competition.

One step in the emergence of the new global humanism which I am seeking to trace has been the opening up to Western scholars and students of fuller knowledge of the great civilized traditions of Asia, notably of India, China, and Japan. The coming of age of this new development has been marked by the establishment of courses in Asian humanities in our colleges and universities. What we of the West are now beginning to see is that there is not one humanism. We have been using the label for Western humanism; but this must be placed in context with the humanism or humanistic traditions of the non-Western world. There are in short as many humanisms as there are civilized bodies of thought in the world. Each of these is a distinctive cluster of values which in effect proposes its own answer to the question put by the man in the middle of our circle. In this connection, it is a fact of some importance that each of the humane traditions of the non-Western world bears a very close relation to the religious tradition of the particular culture.

Let us now take a further step and relate these points to our parable. The people around the circumference of the circle represent the functioning faiths and philosophies of the world—the different value systems which propose their various answers to the questions of the man in the middle. Man puts the existential question, "Why am I alive?" He must then choose among the answers furnished by the value systems, and he must live out his life in terms of his choice.

There are many serious issues raised by the interpretation of the faiths and philosophies of mankind set forth here, and they may well be forming as questions in the reader's mind. Let me anticipate two such questions. First, does humanism permit this new and somewhat wider interpretation? And second, do the traditional faiths or religions of mankind willingly lend themselves to the interpretation just proposed? Both of these questions deserve more detailed answers than is here possible.

In response to the first question, I would like to point out two contrasting interpretations of man which have alternated in the Western tradition, and both of which have their analogues in other traditions. One is Protagoras' view that man is the measure, and the other is Nietzsche's view that man is a bridge, a bridge to something beyond himself. The crucial problem for us is whether humanism is so closely tied to the first view that it has no possible or proper application to the second.

Let me here attempt a reconciliation, which begins with the historical observation that men seem inevitably to serve something bigger and better than themselves or than Man or Humanity. It was

Milton's Satan who declared proudly, "I will not serve." Yet despite his proud boast, Satan did end up serving—and in most unpleasant circumstances. It seems to me a factual observation of man in history that he does not stand alone. The realistic question is then not "Will he serve?" but "What will he serve?"

In order to keep the discussion as neutral and descriptive as possible, let us call man's possible objects of allegiance or service not gods or lords but so many Xs. Let us further state in the light of our previous discussion that the service of some Xs stultifies or dehumanizes man while the service of others has the opposite effect of humanizing him. Paraphrasing and somewhat altering Saint Augustine's dictum, let us posit that there is an X such that the service of X is perfect bondage or servility, but that there is an X such that the service of X is perfect freedom. I would myself not hesitate to say that the difference between a true and a false god, an adequate versus an inadequate view of deity, may be put in terms of the humanizing quality of the true view and the dehumanizing quality of the false.

To return to the issue of humanism versus what may perhaps be called a transhumanistic view of man, the proposal here made is to use the terms *humanizing* and *dehumanizing* as adjectives modifying the faiths men hold. That any man holds some faith seems to me what William James termed a forced option—a situation where one cannot not choose. Men inevitably live by some faith as long as they are men, whether it is Christianity or Judaism or Buddhism or Hinduism or Marxism or Humanism or whatever. I make the proposal to test the faiths men hold by their humanizing quality quite openly and factually. This means that we must all take a fresh look—and continue to take fresh looks—at the faiths or value systems we and others subscribe to in order to see in fact which ones are humanizing and which ones are dehumanizing, and in what ways.

The second and equally hard question is by what right I have construed religions as ways of understanding human existence. The issue can be put in a number of ways. Most directly and bluntly, it may be asked if I have not turned words and ideas upside down. In plain language, traditional religion deals with God or gods; hence to consider it as dealing with human existence is to stand it on its head.

My response is to appeal to the world's primary religious sources or texts, like the Bible and the other sacred books of the world. While I cannot take the space here to make good my case, my contention is that a fair-minded and critical appraisal of these documents and of the faiths which find expression in them shows that they deal centrally and primarily with the nature and destiny of man, with the nature and conduct of man's life. In many of these sources, such as early Buddhism's, the idea of deity is declared to be extraneous, and in some, such as Jainism's, it is specifically denied. Where the idea of deity enters, as in monotheistic religions like Judaism, Christianity, and Islam, it is with reference to the human situation. For example, in the Bible, the term *God* occurs in such statements as "Thus saith the Lord. . . ." And what the Lord says is invariably something about the nature and destiny of man.

To this major evidence drawn from primary religious sources I would add a growing body of evidence from the behavioral sciences, notably anthropology, to the effect that in any culture, religion deals with the values which give meaning and orientation to life within the culture. These values are the human stuff of which the world's religions are made. While anthropological investigation has dealt largely with folk religions or religions of folk societies, I see no reason that these results may not be extended to include the religions of more complex human cultures as well.

If this evidence is accepted, then it follows that the interpretation I am offering does not turn religion upside down but on the contrary turns it right-side up. I would argue that in the modern West, roughly since the Enlightenment, there has been a massive misconception of religion as a hypothesis concerning a remote being called God whose dwelling place is just beyond the reach of our longest-range telescope. Theists accept this hypothesis and atheists and skeptics reject it; but significantly they agree, and I would say mistakenly, in the primary meaning of or reference for religion. I would call this the fallacy of the Head Spirit (I am tempted to say the Head Spook) Out There. What I have said about the primary reference of faith may be understood as an attempt to set this massive misconception right. Once more, for supporting evidence we need only appeal to a free and fair-minded reading of the primary sources of the world's faiths.

There is a fourth and final proposition which must be asserted in order to sustain the argument of this discussion. It is that the values which constitute the human content of the world's faiths are expressed in symbolic forms. Hence, from this standpoint, the world's faiths are so many systems of powerful symbols. By speaking of the world's faiths thus, I am seeking to assert that they are distinctive clusters of imaginative or poetic words and nonverbal symbols which directly communicate light and power to the people who stand within their communities and under their authority.

In terms of their mode of occurrence in the human mind, these symbols are images, or in Whitehead's striking phrase, they occur in the mode of presentational immediacy. They are as it were flashed upon the screen of the mind, and they carry the world's faiths with them to the person to whom they come.

Now, as I have already sought to argue, the human content of these symbol systems is the life values which are offered as answers to the human question. However, it is important to distinguish at this juncture between the observer's viewpoint and the participant's. As students of man's faiths, our proper viewpoint is that of observers, as objective and fair-minded as possible. Such for example is the stance of this chapter. The talk about values—the so-called values language for this whole area of human experience—has its proper and indispensable use as a tool of study and understanding. But it must be pointed out that when we cease to be observers and become participants in any value system, we cease to use an observer's language and begin perforce to speak a sharply contrasting language of powerful expressive symbols. It is in these latter terms that the people around the circumference of the circle address themselves to the man in the middle. It is also important to note in this connection that each of the faiths of the world has an altogether concrete or particular quality. They are not symbols in general or any old symbols but precisely these or those symbols and no other. In other words, each of the persons around the circumference of the circle addressing himself to the man in the middle speaks his own language.

I would like to add some comments about the past and present relations to each other of the people gathered around our circle. As I said at the beginning, historically they have sometimes behaved very badly toward each other. They have bashed each other's heads in and they have cut each other's throats. Some of them have seemed unaware of anybody else standing next to them. Some have behaved badly too in their treatment of the man in the middle, tyrannizing over him and often seeking to pull the wool over his eyes. Small wonder that he has begun to talk back, to respond critically, stating the conditions under which he is willing to listen to their proposals!

Yet I do believe that there are modest grounds for hope in the present situation. At least a few of these people around the circumference are beginning to talk with one another, seeking to learn from the other. There is in other words at least the beginning of dialogue among the world's faiths, and from my experience, I adjudge that there is much to be hoped for in this emerging communication. But this is a subject for another future discussion.

Here let me conclude by stating two principles that may guide the behavior of the people around the circumference in the period of nascent dialogue.

First, each faith is addressed: to whom it may concern. We have argued that all the faiths may legitimately be construed as proposals for the fulfillment or realization of man's humanity, and that they must be considered in the context of man's full human stature of freedom and responsibility. In this context, each faith is, once more, addressed: to whom it may concern.

Second, in the free and open encounter between faiths and of faiths with mankind, let the best faith win. There is and there will continue to be a global competition for the allegiance of men's minds and hearts. This contest is an inexorable fact of life in our times. It is also on balance a good thing, for it will test the vitality and vigor of the competitors. In the encounter, let us simply say again: let the best faith win. And by *best* is meant the most adequate to the human situation.

REV. ROBERT L. FARICY, S.J.

7 The Image of Man in the Writings of Teilhard de Chardin

I

Father Pierre Teilhard de Chardin's writings stretch in time from before World War I to his death in 1955, and in subject matter from physical anthropology to mystical theology. In this vast labyrinth of notes, essays, articles, and books, there is a central point of reference: the problem that is man, the problem of man. Teilhard sees man as a question looking for an answer. More precisely, his thought—scientific, philosophical, and religious—centers about the problem that is man today, seen in the light of his past and as moving into a future, but nevertheless in terms of his contemporary experience. Teilhard finds in the heart of contemporary man the question of the ultimate meaningfulness of human life, of the life of the person and of the totality of mankind.

Man today has faith in the world; he has faith in his species, its progress, its capacity to build the world. But this human faith that is the mark of the modern era is already in crisis; how can it be validated, substantiated, supported? Man today has hope in the future, but it is more and more shaky; how can it be justified and solidified? Further, how can his faith and hope stand up in the face of all the suffering and evil on earth? Contemporary human experience takes the form of a question mark; contemporary man is the problem. In his analysis of contemporary experience, particularly in his understanding of man's faith in progress and his hope in the future, Teilhard outlines the problem of man more clearly, and he points to the solution.

Human faith in man and in his potential for building the world has the characteristics of a religious faith. Modern man has discovered the immensity of things, of the universe, of mankind; he has also discovered the unity of reality, the oneness of the cosmos, the oneness of the human race. He has a coherent world view, that of a world headed as a totality toward some future. "These characteristics define a religion, for the religious dimension appears as soon as the world is seen in its totality and in its ultimate destination," [1] Teilhard writes. And "Whatever may be said, our century is religious. How could it fail to be with such vast horizons opening before it and with such problems to be solved?" [2] "The world has never been more religiously ardent. It is burning now, however, with a new fire, . . . with a faith and a hope that are bound up with the building of the earth." [3]

Contemporary faith in man, in progress, in the future is really a hope. Man's whole orientation today is toward the future; he lives neither in the past nor in the present, but leans forward in time. He is interested in what the future holds, in what is new, and he uses the expression "What's new?" as a common greeting. Because he is future-directed, contemporary man is fundamentally pragmatic; he is interested in what is useful for building the future, in what works. And he speaks pejoratively when he says that something or someone is "useless." Man today views reality as the future to be created; he sees the world as world with possibilities. He is, and he wants to be, involved in the world as a future to be built. This involvement helps him stretch and transcend the limitations of the present and enables him to grow as a person. And his commitment is typically to the future of *this* world, not to some "other world."

The modern "religion of earth," found at its most intense in the blind faith in science and technology that characterized Nazism and fascism and that is basic to communism, is in crisis. [4] It is quite clear that blind faith in progress cannot stand by itself. How, then, can human faith and hope be validated? What are the conditions, the presuppositions, of a solid faith and hope in the world's future?

Faith is relative; ultimately, faith is relative to persons. At bottom, I can believe and trust only in a person. If I am to have faith in the

---

[1] "Quelques Réflexions sur la conversion du monde," *Science et Christ*, vol. IX of *Oeuvres de Pierre Teilhard de Chardin*, Paris, Éditions du Seuil, 1965, p. 158.

[2] Letter of December 10, 1952, quoted in Claude Cuénot, *Teilhard de Chardin*, tr. Vincent Colimore, Baltimore, Helicon Press, 1965, p. 368.

[3] "Christianisme et évolution," unpublished essay written in 1954, ms., pp. 1–2.

[4] See "La Mystique de la science," *L'Énergie humaine*, vol. VI of *Oeuvres de Pierre Teilhard de Chardin*, Paris, Éditions du Seuil, 1962, pp. 203–223.

world, then I must somehow understand the world in personal terms.
If my faith in the world is to stand firm, be justified, then I must
see the world as somehow grounded in the personal. Hope, too, is
relative, not only to the future but to persons. Hope depends, seeks
help, reaches out. If I hope, then, ultimately I must hope in some*one*.
Faith and hope are necessarily interpersonal attitudes; they presuppose a certain personal mutuality. To believe or to hope means to
be somehow mutual with; and again, a person can only be mutual
with other persons. This, then, leads to the first part of the question
posed by contemporary human experience: how can the world that
is moving into the future be seen as rooted in the personal?

What is more, contemporary faith in progress and hope in the
future are threatened by the lack of guarantee that there will be a
future at all. Faith in the world's future is being eaten away by an
indefinable fear, by a specifically modern general anxiety. "Something threatens us, something is more than ever lacking, but without
our being able to say exactly what." [5] There is something "that
brings a restless uneasiness to individuals and to nations." [6] Mankind
is the one species that converges in its evolution; and this evolutionary convergence has sharply accelerated in modern times. With the
population explosion, the rise of technology, and the communications revolution, the human species has entered into the compressive
phase of its evolution, into a phase of rapid socialization. The result is
that solitude and quiet are disappearing, people are more and more
crowded together, persons are increasingly lost in the bigness and
the complexity of institutions. In the face of these pressures, man
is nervous and afraid. He is afraid with an existential fear the roots
of which are in human consciousness itself; but it is an anxiety that
is greater and has a more acute quality today than in past ages.[7]

What is precisely the fear that erodes man's hope? It is the fear of
death, Teilhard suggests, not the death of the individual but the
death of the species. It is the fear that mankind's rapid progress
will end in nothing. It is the "sickness of the dead end, the anguish

[5] *The Phenomenon of Man*, tr. Bernard Wall, 2nd ed., New York, Harper &
Row, Publishers, Harper Torchbook, 1965, p. 226.
[6] *Man's Place in Nature*, tr. René Hague, New York, Harper & Row, Publishers, 1966, p. 103.
[7] Teilhard analyzes contemporary anxiety in several essays; see particularly
"Un Phénomène de contre-évolution en biologie humaine ou la peur de l'existence," *L'Activation de l'énergie*, vol. VII of *Oeuvres de Pierre Teilhard de
Chardin*, Paris, Éditions du Seuil, 1963, pp. 189–202.

of feeling shut in." [8] In the past century, man has become conscious of evolution, of living in an evolutionary world. He is caught up in society's evolutionary progress, and his fear is that mankind's course will not have a successful outcome, that there is no way out of the universe, that human evolution is headed toward a point of no return, a dead end. Toward the end of his life Teilhard wrote: "Is it not this presentiment of a blank wall ahead, underlying all other tensions and specific fears, which paradoxically (at the very moment when every barrier seems to be giving way before our power of understanding and mastering the world) is darkening and hardening the minds of our generation?" [9] It might be objected that the human species could drag on in time and spread itself indefinitely, that it could run down more and more. "But is this not the precise opposite of what is happening here and now in the human world?" [10] No, mankind is a species which converges, which does not dissipate itself but concentrates, folds in, upon itself.

The question, then, is this: is there, for man, light at the end of the tunnel? Is there a suitable outcome, outlet, for mankind? The fear that the tunnel might be closed is the core of the contemporary anxiety. If man is to continue to hope in the future, then he has to have a guarantee that there will be a future, an ultimate future, a way out. For this is hope's function: to hypothesize, to imagine, to search for ways out. Hope desires and wants and wishes *because* it can imagine future possibilities and solutions. Hope looks to the next step, looks to progress, gives man motion into the future. Man moves into the future to the degree that he has hope. Hopelessness, on the other hand, paralyzes, immobilizes, keeps man in the present, stops him. And uncertainty about the future is what gives contemporary man fear, what makes him hesitate. If man's hope is to continue, if human hope in the future is to be supported, then man must have a guarantee of the ultimately successful outcome of human progress, a guarantee of an ultimate future.

In sum, then, the question posed by contemporary human experience is twofold: how can the world be understood as personal so that man can have faith in the world; and how can the future be known as ultimately successful so that man can have hope in it? This

[8] *The Phenomenon of Man*, p. 228.
[9] "The End of the Species," *The Future of Man*, tr. Norman Denny, New York, Harper & Row, Publishers, 1964, p. 300.
[10] *Ibid.*, p. 301.

dual problem is compounded by the apparently increasing evil in the
world: how can man have human faith and hope in the face of so
much suffering, war, untimely death, hatred, malice?

II

Teilhard de Chardin tries to formulate for man today the peren-
nial Christian answer to the question inherent in contemporary experience. The solution to the problem of man is Christ risen. It is in
the person of the risen Christ that the world is rooted; it is Christ
who assures the world's ultimate future; it is Christ who by his death
and resurrection has conquered evil. It is Christ risen who justifies
and gives solidity to man's faith in the world and to his hope in the
future.

Human faith in the world and in man's effort to build up the
world is possible because the world is grounded in the person of
Christ. It is here that Christian faith goes beyond and fulfills human
faith, and it is this that being a Christian adds to being human. Man
can be interpersonally mutual with the world, have faith in the
world, because the world is centered on a Person. Teilhard habitually
writes of Christ as the personal Center of the cosmos. "Besides those
attributes which are strictly divine and human (those attributes to
which theologians have paid the most attention up to now), Christ
possesses—in virtue of the working out of the implications of his
incarnation—attributes which are 'universal,' 'cosmic,' attributes
which show him to be the world's personal Center." [11] "The common Center of things, Christ can be loved as a person, and he presents himself as a world." [12] The risen Christ can be considered
either as "the Center toward whom all things converge or the milieu
in which they exist. . . . Christ has not only a mystical Body but
also a *cosmic Body* (of which it is Saint Paul who describes the chief
characteristics)." [13] "To the Christian . . . it is above all Christ who
invests himself with the whole reality of the universe; but at the
same time it is the universe which is illumined with all the warmth
and immortality of Christ." [14]

The Christ to whom Teilhard points, the cosmic Christ who makes

[11] "Quelques Réflexions sur la conversion du monde," p. 161.
[12] "Le Prêtre," *Science et Christ*, pp. 292–293.
[13] "L'Union créatrice," *Écrits du temps de la guerre (1916–1919)*, Paris,
Bernard Grasset, 1965, pp. 196–197; see also the English of this work, *Writings
in Time of War*, tr. René Hague, New York, Harper & Row, Publishers, 1968.
[14] "Turmoil or Genesis," *The Future of Man*, p. 224.

faith in the world possible because he is its organic Center, is the Christ of Saint John, Saint Paul, and the Greek fathers of the Church. He is God's creative Word through whom all things have come to be and in whom they exist; he is the personal principle of the order and harmony and existence of all things, in whom all things are reconciled. ". . . in him all things hold together," and "in him all things find their fulfillment," in such a way that "Christ is all things and in all." [15] He is the Christ in whom all creation is recapitulated, the Pantocrator. He is, moreover, contemporary man's "unknown God" to whom human faith in the world points and who makes that faith possible and personal.

Faith in Christ completes and gives substance to faith in the world; and hope in the risen Christ completes and gives substance to hope in the future. The ultimately successful outcome of progress, of human evolution, is guaranteed in the resurrection of Christ. Christ risen is the guarantee of the ultimate future of the world; he is the guarantor that the world will not finish in a dead end but in a transformation and a new beginning. He is the certain assurance that there is a way out of the universe; he is the light at the end of the tunnel. "In a world that is with certainty open at its summit in Christ Jesus, man no longer risks dying of suffocation." [16] "For the Christian, the eventual success of man on earth is not merely a probability but a certainty, since Christ (and in Him, by anticipation, the world) is already risen." [17] By his own resurrection Christ has become, in himself, the existential structure of the world's resurrection, the personal guarantor of the transformation of this world, and the guarantor of its ultimate glorious future. Christ risen, and only he, can shore up human hope in the future; for he contains in himself, by anticipation, the ultimate future. The risen Christ *is* the world's ultimate future. Hope in Christ, then, makes possible and justifies human hope. For the Christian, hope in Christ and hope in the future are one hope.

The world moving into the future can be believed in, hoped in, and loved because it is grounded in Christ risen, the guarantor of its ultimately successful outcome. It is true that there is suffering in the world, and hardship, wars, hatred, death. But Christ has overcome these by his cross and resurrection. It is true that, in a world in

---

[15] Col. 1:17, 2:10, 3:11; see "Mon Univers," *Science et Christ*, p. 84.
[16] "Le Christique," unpublished essay written in 1955, ms., p. 7.
[17] "The Directions and Conditions of the Future," *The Future of Man*, p. 237.

progress, in a world which is not yet finished, disorder and failure are inevitable at every level—suffering and death at the physical level, ignorance at the intellectual level, sin at the moral level. Evil is a statistical necessity in a universe that is in process toward greater unification. Christ, however, by his resurrection, has taken the sting out of evil, has overcome it. By his redemptive death on the cross, Christ has raised up the world, "an act of expiation, but also a hard journey of conquest." [18] Christ has made of suffering and death the passage to resurrection, the way—through metamorphosis—to the ultimate future. In this life, man is in the structure of the cross, but it is a cross pointed toward resurrection. For Teilhard, the cross "is the symbol, the way, the very act of progress." [19] It is the symbol of victory through difficult labor, of "the creative but laborious effort of mankind climbing toward Christ who awaits it." [20]

The answer, then, to the question contained in contemporary human experience is the cross and resurrection of Christ; the answer is Christ who has died and who has been raised up. More precisely, the answer is the risen Christ in his saving relation to man. The solution to the problem of man is Christ risen as containing in himself man's own ultimate future. The image of man in Teilhard's writings is, first, man as problem, man whose human faith and human hope are in need of Christ. Balancing this image and complementing it is Teilhard's image of the inauguration of man's promised future, his image of man and of the world at the second coming of Christ, at the parousia. Teilhard does not expect God to truncate the work that he has begun; the world will not end until it is finished, has been built up to a point of maximum maturity. Christ will not come a second time until the world is prepared for his coming, until mankind has reached the maximum point of its progress. And yet, that man build the earth to a maximum is only a necessary condition of the parousia, not a sufficient condition. The transformation of the world at Christ's second coming will be an act of God in the strict sense of the word, a divine intervention that will mark the death and metamorphosis of the world we know into the world God has promised us in Christ's resurrection.

What will be the condition of man after the parousia? It will be a

[18] "Quelques Vues générales sur l'essence du Christianisme," unpublished essay written in 1939, ms., p. 2.

[19] "The New Spirit," *The Future of Man*, p. 95.

[20] "Intégration de l'homme dans l'univers," unpublished essay written in 1930, ms., p. 13.

state that we can understand now only dimly, and through symbols and images. But we do know that it will be a condition of maximum union of men with one another and centered on Christ. We know that it will be a final synthesis of the world and God in Christ, a reconciliation in Christ. Persons will be achieved and fulfilled, not despite the intensity of the union in Christ but because of it. In any union, the elements united are differentiated, and in a union of persons, the persons are further personalized. In teams, in friendship, in marriage, the person finds his own growth as a person through union with others. This is above all true of union with Christ; at his second coming, he will take men to himself and so unite them more closely among themselves and personalize them to the highest degree possible.

Teilhard de Chardin never writes of Christ considered simply in himself. Christ is understood always as the organic Center of the world and as the focal point of its evolution; Christ is understood in terms of the world's relation to him and, more exactly, of man's relation to him. Because Teilhard habitually considers Christ in relation to man and to the world, the eucharist has a central place in his theology. The Christ who is the answer to human faith and human hope because he is the focal Center of reality, the Christ who grounds in himself man's world and who contains in himself man's ultimate future, is the same Christ who is actively present in the eucharist. Christ present for man is above all Christ present in the eucharist. In the eucharist "is truly lodged the Center of Christ's personal energy." [21] It is through his saving action in the eucharist that Christ unites man to himself in personalizing union, and through man the world. It is the eucharistic Christ who centers the world on himself and gives it a face, and who makes present now—in himself—man's ultimate future. Teilhard finds the world at its most personal, and the promised future present now, in the eucharistic Christ. The solution to the problem that man is is the risen Christ eucharistically present for man.

III

For us today, several years after Teilhard de Chardin's death, Christ is still the answer to the question that is man. The task of theology is to interpret God's revelation to man in the categories of contemporary experience so that God's saving revelation can be

[21] "Mon Univers," p. 91.

communicated. The fullness of that saving revelation is the risen Christ; he himself is what must be understood and communicated by the theology teacher.

It is clear that theology today is alive, moving, vigorous. It is equally clear that in many instances it does not have Christ for the center of its reflection and the content of its communication. *Much that passes for theology is simply humanism,* merely a formulation of the human question without an effort to communicate the answer that is Christ. More: there is much theologizing that seems to serve primarily to gratify the emotional needs of the theologizer rather than to proclaim Christ, that seems designed to shock, startle, appear liberal and progressive, win praise, gain esteem. The danger is a new dishonesty that would use theology to rationalize personal compromises and then teach the compromises as truth. Considerable harm is being done by theology that dilutes Christ and his meaning for man, that distorts Christ in the name of relevance or progress. There are several examples of the new dishonesty: exhibitionism in the name of holy disobedience, the justification of underground liturgies in the name of freedom, the theological discounting of mental prayer in the name of secularity and incarnationalism, the condoning of abortion in the name of compassion, the watering down of Christ's eucharistic presence in the name of humanism and community.

Teilhard de Chardin's legacy serves to remind us that there is one truth to be taught. It is Christ crucified, dead, buried, and risen in glory to be the foundation of man's faith and hope and the personal center of his love.

IV Images for Action

PETER G. AHR

8 Christian Faith and Faith Statements

One of the major problems facing the Church today is that of the meaning of faith. This problem appears in such varied guises as the demythologization controversy; the attempts to restate the Church's belief which marked the "death of God" school; the increasing interest of religious circles in the phenomenon of atheism, most recently evidenced in the establishment of an official Vatican secretariat for dialogue with nonbelievers; and the lively debates which followed the publication of such books as Leslie Dewart's *The Future of Belief* and Charles Davis' *A Question of Conscience*. Out of this ferment have come several generally accepted answers as well as perhaps a larger number of questions. I would hope here to indicate some of each, with a few observations on how the questions may be answerable.

One of the results of contemporary discussions on faith is the recognition that any question about the nature of faith is dealing with either or both of two rather distinct objects: faith as the existential act of the believer, and the statements made about faith by the individual believer or the believing community. In other words, we recognize that it is one thing to believe in God and another to say, "I believe in God." Either may exist without the other, although normally (that is, ideally, but not necessarily in the majority of cases) they exist together in the individual. The faith necessary for salvation can occur outside the believing community of the Church, and not everyone who says, "Lord, Lord," will enter the Kingdom of Heaven. But neither of these situations, although together they may describe the majority of the human race, can be regarded as the norm for theological discussion. The problem which interests us here is, what is a man doing when he believes, and what is he doing

when he says that he believes, and that he believes in God? And how
do these two relate to each other?

First of all, then, what is faith as an existential act of man? It is
certainly not basically an intellectual act, a mere assent to propositions which are accepted as true. It is rather a response of the whole
person—as a whole and not as a conglomerate of intellect, will, and
body—to the God who is seen to reveal himself. It is an attitude
which the individual takes to the whole of reality, a stance which
consists ultimately in a setting of priorities, in a hierarchy of values
by which he (and the believing community) lives. At the summit of
this hierarchy stands one value, one object, to which the individual
accords what Paul Tillich describes as "ultimate concern." It is this
object that the individual defines himself in terms of: "I exist for
this; my activity is basically directed to this; the attaining or possession of this is what I feel will insure my happiness." This basic structure of faith is the same whatever the object of the faith, be it
wealth, power, sex, freedom, or God.[1]

Or is it? Is faith (at least Christian faith) actually structured in
this way? Is the God of the Judeo-Christian revelation one who presents himself to man as the object of this kind of faith attitude? Certainly, traditional theology has tended to speak of God and faith
in basically this way. Indeed, the project of a *theo-logia*, of a "speaking about God," would seem to presuppose that God can be spoken
of as an object, can be made to be the subject of affirmations that are
understood to be "about" him. Religion, too, is customarily understood as a form of search for God, as a way of contacting the God
who is believed to make himself the object of this human search,
however divinely assisted this search is thought to be. The believer
is encouraged to shape his life as a religious quest, whose term will
be, he hopes, the eternal beatitude of the possession of God. It is
basically assumed that everyone knows who this God is, what the
word *God* refers to. The use of such descriptions as "Supreme
Being," "Creator," "Father" at least gives the impression that we
all know what we are talking about and that we are all talking about
the same thing.

But do we know, in fact, what we are talking about? Do we
know what the word *God* means? The question is a serious one, and
one which cannot be answered simply by an appeal to the inade-

[1] For a discussion of how such absolutes function as god substitutes in a
nonreligious faith, see Arthur Gibson, *The Faith of the Atheist,* New York,
Harper & Row, Publishers, 1968.

quacy of human knowledge or by a discussion of the nature of analogical knowledge, however useful these may be. For in the Bible and in a significant but little-heeded area of Christian tradition, we are faced with a God who precisely escapes our concepts and our language. Indeed, the most arresting feature of the God of the Old and New Testaments is his unpredictability, his refusal to live up to the religious expectations of his people.

The God of Old Testament revelation is the God who refuses to give Moses his name[2] and therefore does not furnish his worshiper with a direct way of addressing him—he keeps his phone number unlisted, as it were, and does not allow his presence to be commanded, as one who knew the divine name would expect it to be. He is the God who creates, not by slaying the dragon of chaos and forming the world out of its corpse the way a potter makes a jar by destroying the "formlessness" of the clay, and not by begetting it with or without the aid of a divine consort (any one of which processes are intelligible enough, and the sort of creating expressed in the myths of the Hebrews' neighbors and hence presumably the way the Hebrews would have expected God to have created the world), but simply by commanding that things be. He is the God who forbids any images to be made of him: who forbids, therefore, any attempts to concretize him and to tie him down to any place or form. He is the God who says of the religious observances prescribed by the Law:

> What to me is the multitude of your sacrifices?
>   says the Lord;
> I have had enough of burnt offerings of rams
>   and the fat of fed beasts;
> I do not delight in the blood of bulls,
>   or of lambs, or of he-goats.[3]

The examples could be multiplied, but the point should already be clear: the God revealed in the Old Testament is a God who refuses to act as a god would be expected to. The Hebrews' contemporaries had certain clear notions of what the gods were like,

---

[2] Ex. 3:14. The point is the same, no matter how God's "answer" is translated and understood. "I am who I am, period" is no more an answer to Moses' question than is "I am who am." "I will be what I will be" and "I cause to be what I cause to be" are equally refusals to answer the question, as is "I am who I am for you." In any case, Moses walks away from the encounter no wiser about God's name than he was before, no more able to command his presence by invoking his secret name.

[3] Is. 1:11.

notions which the Hebrews shared. But Yahweh is not like any of these gods, to such an extent that the common notion of "god" is not really applicable to him. The Old Testament discloses the difficulties the Hebrews had with this intractable God: their recurrent attempts to assimilate the worship of other gods into worship of him, the deuteronomic codification of him and his demands, and the prophetic insistence on the fact that this God is simply not like the other gods.

It is this prophetic tradition that Jesus is closest to; this same ungodlike God, this same God who does not fit the common notion of what a god is and how a god acts is the one whom Jesus reveals and speaks of as his Father. The whole perspective of realized eschatology uncovered by modern exegesis compels us to recognize to what extent Jesus broke with his contemporaries' religious expectations by throwing askew their entire historical understanding of God's intervention in history. "The Kingdom of God is among you," he said, but there were no angels with trumpets, no empirical evidence of the advent of the Kingdom. Jesus' willingness to break the Law at times, his consorting with publicans and sinners were proof to the "religious" that he could not have been sent by God. Again, then, we are faced in Jesus with a God who does not fit the categories of what is and what is not acceptable divine behavior. We Christians should therefore beware of saying too easily that we know what that word *God* means, since the very revelation on which we base ourselves teaches us that we cannot know what God is, or to put it more exactly, that our idea of God is more than likely wrong. For the God of the Bible is a God who is none too careful to conform with our notions of what he ought to be.

Christian faith, therefore, whatever it is, must be a faith in this God who is thus sovereignly free, thus absolutely beyond all our comprehension and unlike all our ideas of him. Consequently, the faith response to this sort of God cannot be the same as a faith in anything else. For faith of the garden-variety sort presupposes that the object of faith is "there" to be sought after. The object—be it wealth or power or even a god—must be clearly enough seen for the believer to be able to direct his actions toward it and perhaps even recognize it if he finds it. But how can this happen with a God who refuses on principle to be seen as God at all?

Faith indeed is an attitude to reality taken as a kind of response to some one object. But the faith response to the God who reveals himself in the Bible must be conditioned by the fact that there is in this case no conceivable object to respond to. The God whom Christians worship is a God not made by human hands—or by human minds. He is a God who to man is silent, in a way that is strikingly evoked by Ingmar Bergman's film *Winter Light*. Pastor Tomas Eriksson finds himself close to despair over the breakdown of his ability to find the God whom he has used to preach love to his congregation and his wife, to assuage the anxiety of the troubled, and to console the sorrowing. At the close of the film, he is cornered in the sacristy by the crippled old sexton, who speaks to him of Jesus' suffering:

ALGOT: But think of Gethsemane, Vicar. All his disciples asleep. They hadn't understood a thing, not the last supper, nothing. . . . Vicar, that must have been a terrible suffering! To understand that no one has understood you. To be abandoned when one really needs someone to rely on. A terrible suffering.

TOMAS [*after a pause*]: Yes. Obviously.

ALGOT: Well. But that wasn't the worst thing, even so! When Christ had been nailed up on the cross and hung there in his torments, he cried out: "God, my God, why hast thou forsaken me?" He cried out as loud as he possibly could. He thought his Father in Heaven had abandoned him. He believed everything he'd been preaching was a lie. The moments before he died, Christ was seized with a great doubt. Surely that must have been his most monstrous suffering of all? I mean God's silence. Isn't that true, Vicar? [4]

Faced with the same doubt, with the same silence, Tomas orders the beginning of Vespers, enters the sanctuary, and intones: "Holy, holy, holy, Lord God almighty. All the earth is full of his glory." The palpable absence of the expected God is the real presence of the holy God. All his life, Tomas has been believing in an understandable God; but the God who is holy is the God whom understanding doubts.

Belief in this God is therefore really a nonbelief in that which we can understand. Or to put it another way, if we can even conceive of it, it is not God. In the final analysis, the Christian is called on not to believe in any thing, that is, not to make any tangible or conceivable object the reference point of his ultimate concern. His life of faith is indeed an attitude toward reality, an attitude of response to what is central to his life. But he does not know what that

---

[4] Ingmar Bergman, *Three Screenplays: "Through a Glass Darkly," "The Communicants" ("Winter Light"), and "The Silence,"* New York, Orion Press, 1965, p. 101.

central point is; he knows only what it is not: it is not anything that he can conceive of. In the language of John of the Cross, at the summit of the mountain of prayer there is *nothing*. To say, "I believe in God," then, is to say, "I am a response to what I cannot name; no thing can take the central place in my life"—a curious but reassuring parallel to the first commandment. The act which is faith can have no perceivable object; but it is testified to precisely by the absence of any object in the place of God in the believer's life.

It is in this way that faith can be truly liberating, for the absence of any overriding object or value in the believer's life enables him to see all things as less than ultimately important and therefore as objects of real choice. This is the function of that demythologization of the cosmos which the Old Testament belief in God evidences. The prophets' denunciations of the Canaanite fertility cult, for example, serve precisely to say: "Sex and fertility are not divine powers to be contacted by means of worship; they too are creatures of the God whom we worship. He is the only one who deserves worship; they are but things to be lived and used." In the same way, belief in this God frees us from attaching any overriding, worship-inducing importance to any of the elements of our experience.

At this point, however, we run into a serious difficulty. The very prophets who proclaim the absolute transcendence of God do so with the formula, "Thus says the Lord." The unthinkability of God is phrased in concepts; the ineffable is (and must be) spoken of. Here we are at the heart of the paradox of religious language: we must speak in positive terms of that which is, for us, functionally negative. The problem is not a new one, but it is one to which theology is again paying close attention. We can formulate it in this way: Christian faith is at bottom a preverbal attitude of denying ultimate concern to any tangible object (hence, functionally negative); but it cannot be experienced or conveyed to others without being put into language made up of positive statements (for the piling up of negative statements is ultimately an exercise in non-communication, as the reader may now feel after following the foregoing attempt to evoke the sheer negativity of the act of faith).

How, then, can we make positive statements about this basically negative act? How can we verify such statements? What criterion can we use to say that they are true? Ordinary positive statements, such as "The chair is brown," "It is ten o'clock," and "I am sick," presuppose that there is something knowable (and presumably known) about the chair, the time, or my health. The statements are said to be true insofar as they adequately express what is known about the chair, the time, or my health. But what is the "known" that can validate a statement of faith?

In answering this question, we must first of all note that there are two kinds of faith statements: the dogmatic and the moral. The latter take the form "God commands [or forbids] X," and correspond with the actions in which the faith attitude is concretized in the believer's life. The former either are reducible to or immediately take the form "God [or Christ or the Church or whatever] is X," and provide the theoretical underpinning of the moral actions. The two types of statements are different, and should call for somewhat different kinds of verification.

We must also note this characteristic of positive statements, that they are answers to implied or explicit questions and can therefore be judged true or false only insofar as they answer these questions. Thus, the statement "The chair is brown" answers the question "What color is that particular chair?" If we are in fact talking about a green chair, the statement must be said to be false, however logically consistent it may be within itself.

What, then, is the "known" of dogmatic statements, and how can they be verified? It is already clear that this "known" cannot be God himself. I would suggest, however, that it is to be found in the basic faith attitude, in that some things cannot be said without compromising or altering this basic faith. Let us take an example.

Christianity says that "God is one." How do we base this statement? Not on a simple appeal to the presence of the same statement in Scripture or in the decrees of the Council of Nicaea, as if these sources contained a direct positive revelation statement from God himself to the effect that he is one; for such an appeal would presuppose an impossibly literal understanding of inspiration which would in turn pay insufficient attention to the ultimate mystery of God and to the real function of the human writers of these words. Rather, the statement "God is one" is the answer given by the biblical author, the Fathers of Nicaea, and the individual believer to the question "How many is God?" or "Is God one or many?" The question in turn has certain presuppositions, particularly that to answer "Many" would demand that one could distinguish among the many—in other words, that one knows enough about God to tell the difference between one and the other. But the basic faith attitude is that God is not known in this way at all. Therefore, the only possible answer to this question which will preserve the Christian faith in God intact is that God is one. The statement is made and called true not because it can be positively verified by reference to some previously known thing but because it is the least inadequate possible answer to the question. Any other answer either would be completely untrue to faith or would at least lead to more difficulties than this one.[5]

Dogmatic statements, then, are verifiable by attending to the relative compatibility or incompatibility of faith with the various possible answers to the question which is being asked of faith. The least inadequate answer is the one which is termed true. By way of parenthesis, we may note here that a full treatment of this theme would call for a discussion of the Spirit's role in the formulation of faith statements and of ecclesiastical and papal infallibility. Such a discussion would speak of the role of the Spirit as divinely assisting in the discernment of the degree of compatibility of faith with the various possible answers to the question actually being asked, and would present infallibility as the divine guarantee that the answer chosen is indeed the one least incompatible with faith.

This understanding of the way in which dogmatic statements are actually made also serves to explain how a large section of the Church can reject a position which later is seen to be orthodox, as with the condemnation of Thomas Aquinas shortly after his death, or uphold a position which is later rejected as heretical (heresy, on this reading, is basically an inadequate answer to the question being asked), as with the Roman Church's teaching of monarchianism in the third and fourth centuries and the condemnation of Origen at the Fifth Ecumenical Council. The change is basically ascribable to the fact that the question itself or its presuppositions have changed in the interim. Thus, the Romans in the third century could see a trinitarian doctrine only as an attack on the uniqueness of God, and therefore denied it, whereas the Greeks and later on the Romans did not see trinitarianism as in any way denying the uniqueness of God, and therefore defended it. Origen's answers were indeed adequate to the questions of the third century; but taken verbally, they created far too many problems for the sixth century, so that his formulations had to be rejected.

The verification of moral statements is similar to that of dog-

[5] For a similar analysis of the great Christological dogmas, see the chapter "The Road to Chalcedon" in Paul Van Buren's *The Secular Meaning of the Gospel*, New York, Harper & Row, Publishers, 1965.

matic statements, but it is complicated by the fact that morality, dealing as it does with concrete actions, is influenced by other factors than just Christian faith. Our attitude toward concrete actions is conditioned at least in part by the way in which our culture regards these actions. In other words, evaluation of moral statements demands attention not only to the framework of the question but also to the presuppositions of the answerer. As the question changes and as the answerer changes, the answer may very well change from one place or time to another; and each answer may be called true.

Let us take as an example of this problem the statement "God forbids war." The question to which this statement is an answer is something like "Is the Christian faith attitude compatible with war?" The answer will in turn be influenced by what the questioner understands war to be and by the degree to which the Christian faith attitude influences his behavior. Thus, a member of Charlemagne's court, brought up on the notion that war is a glorious and noble profession, would be asking, "Is Christian faith compatible with this noble activity?" On the other hand, a modern college student, whose upbringing has placed less stress on the glory of war and more on its sheer wastefulness, would be asking, "Is Christian faith compatible with this sort of destruction?" Already, then, it should be clear that the question, while verbally perhaps the same, is really quite different in the two cases.

In addition to this difference in the question, there is also a difference possible in the degree to which the Christian faith attitude influences the questioner. For the Christian attitude is rarely if ever the only influence on the individual's or the community's stances. There are also a whole series of other cultural currents which combine to shape the individual's view of particular actions, and the relative importance of each factor varies from person to person. Thus, one of Charlemagne's barons whose father or grandfather might have worshiped Wotan could be presumed to have been less influenced by Christianity than his bishop, who had at least devoted his life to religion. Similarly, a major munitions manufacturer might be presumed to be more influenced in this question by non-Christian influences than someone who does not have a similar investment in war.

Given such a complexity, then, how do we verify the moral statement? In this case, I would suggest that verification must take the form of identifying the precise question and the degree to which the Christian faith has molded the answers given to it. Thus, Charlemagne's baron's acceptance of warfare can itself be given little weight while his acceptance of a "truce of God" can, precisely because the latter can be explained only by the entrance of a Christian value formation into his judgment. Charlemagne's bishop's insistence on such a truce is likewise a visible entrance of faith into the question. And when we can find a similar difference in the answers given to the various forms of the question in various times and places, then we can proceed to answer our question today. Again, the answer can be only the least inadequate answer to the question; we can determine this by comparing our possible answers with the least inadequate ones found by past generations of Christians. The answer for us may not indeed agree verbally with those of previous generations, but if our faith answer is the same as theirs in that it too is the least inadequate one to the question being asked, then it can be called true.

To say that our answer is true, however, is not to say that previous different answers have been false. It is simply anachronistic, for example, to condemn Bernard of Clairvaux for preaching a crusade; the crusade was in his time perhaps the best possible solution to the question of war as his time saw it. All we can say is that we cannot preach crusades today.

These considerations can also throw some light on the current controversy surrounding the encyclical *Humanae vitae*. All too often, it seems, assent to or dissent from it is put in the wrong terms. The encyclical is assented to on the premise that the moral formulations of Pius XI or Saint Augustine are automatically valid answers to the modern question of birth control; it is dissented from on the ground that "The Pope has no business in the bedroom" or "His solution does not answer my problem."

In fact, neither reaction is legitimate. This kind of assent does no justice to the possibility that Augustine's or Pius XI's question is not our question. Whether the questions are the same cannot be determined *a priori;* it can be discovered only by a careful examination of what precisely Pius XI's question was and what precisely ours is. Moreover, this kind of assent does not take into consideration the possibility that birth control itself may have meant something to Pius XI and his question that it does not mean to us and ours.

Likewise, the objection that the Pope has no right to speak at all on the question of birth control is an invalid one. For if Christian faith is something which is concretized in action, then the Christian community, of which the Pope is spokesman, does have the right to say whether given actions are compatible with the faith attitude. But this enunciation can only be in terms of the least inadequate answer to the question which is put to it. *Humanae vitae* can only be an answer to the question which it attempts to answer: to judge it as insufficient because it does not provide an adequate answer to a different question is to raise a pointless objection. What that question is can be discovered only by attentive investigation; but it is only in those terms that the encyclical can be validly judged.

Such an investigation still leaves open the possibility that the encyclical's question is itself an inadequate one and thus perforce gives rise to unnecessarily inadequate answers. If this is in fact the case (and such an argument seems to be at the root of much criticism of the document), then a legitimate objection can be made against the encyclical; but the criticism, if it is to be constructive, must be an attempt at refining and improving the question, not a sterile attack on the answer.

For the history of the development of doctrine has been the history of the refining of the questions which the Christian community has put to its faith. And the better the questions have become, the less inadequate has become our understanding and articulation of our wordless faith in the God who speaks to us in silence.

VINCENT ZAMOYTA

9 On Humanae vitae:
A Search for Human Understanding

The Church's timely concern for rapprochement to the world, so eminently realized in the determinations of Vatican II, has brought it to its first great postconciliar crisis. As a child for the first time walks slowly and hesitantly into the water from the beach and, thrown by an unexpectedly large wave, finds itself struggling to regain its balance, so has the Church found itself unsteadied by world reaction to Pope Paul's encyclical "Concerning Human Life."

The child tumbled by the wave will react either with a fearful flight back to securer ground or with buoyant recovery to a stability necessary to face the waves yet to come. In these parlous times, will the Church stand up to the world wave and meet it on its own ground or retreat, worsened by the initial challenge of the modern world?

Perspective

In the interests of obtaining a better perspective on the issue of the encyclical, one could ask: what is "Concerning Human Life" about? It is not sufficient to state that it discusses the morality of artificial birth control. Basically, the encyclical concerns something to which artificial birth control is only related, as being but one application of a general principle which seems to underlie the entire encyclical. From this viewpoint, the document tells mankind more than just that artificial means of birth control are immoral.

We live today on the verge of a new era for humanity. Man has come into possession of forces which will make all human living radically different from what it has ever been. Until now man pretty much had to respect nature and its laws. He recognized that conformity with nature in matters concerning human life, for example, had to be his guideline for fostering it and preserving it. The biologist as experimenter and the physician as healer followed where nature led. They had to look to nature to learn what they must do and how they must do it.

This condition is now on the threshold of being reversed. The meteoric advance of scientific experimentation and technological expertise have given into man's hands a power over life which was heretofore unimagined. No longer confined to a humble respect for his limitations in the face of nature, man now has within his reach the possibility of determining what it can be and become. He has always exercised his dominion over his environment, that part of nature by which he is surrounded, by manipulating it for his own purposes. Man today is beginning to exercise sovereignty over the fundamental constitution and conditions of the human life which is within him. Formerly limited by the specifications of nature, he can now determine those specifications.

This is the most tremendous and consequential power that has ever become the responsibility of man. It gives rise to a dangerous temptation to become Lord of Life. The first glimpses of the possibilities of the science of genetics have opened spectacular prospects for the determination and manipulation of human life. They leave man more breathless than did his first vision of the heliocentric universe, Einsteinian space, the Freudian dimensions of the human mind, or the atomic world. In Japan, scientists extract animal embryos, manipulate them, and return them to living bodies; in Great Britain, scientists have taken a living cell from the intestinal tissue of a frog and from it have produced another frog asexually. How soon will man begin to transfer these techniques to man? Moral issues will arise in the near future which will make the problem of artificial birth control almost ridiculously insignificant. Is not the major importance of Pope Paul's "Concerning Human Life" that fact that it constitutes a responsible caution to man as he enters the world of human life itself to master and direct it at will?

Another factor to consider in an attempt to put "Concerning Human Life" in proper focus is the fact that it concerns sex. Might not part of the adverse reaction to it be conditioned by that preoccupation with sex which is so much a part of the American way of life? For one who is persuaded that life is neither successful nor even worth living unless it is successful in terms of physical love, to one who would identify sex with love, to such a one the conclusions and reasonings of this encyclical cannot be otherwise than unac-

ceptable. To the degree that a Catholic Christian has been affected
or infected by such attitudes, he would find abstinence incomprehensible, rhythm untenable, and the mind of the Pope perverse. (It
is precisely a response like this which reveals to what degree the
Catholic Christian mind has capitulated to "this perverse generation"
of our day.)

Also, the obsession with sex and the consequent vehemence of
the reaction has tended to blow up the question beyond due propor-
tion. One would get the impression, from the impetuosity of the
reaction, that this is the most important and critical issue in the lives
of individuals or humanity in general or in the Church. It is, for
those who tend to absolutize sex in human love. But related to the
entire spectrum of human concern and values, it does not rank as
the world's or the Church's foremost problem. Of much greater
importance and seriousness is the problem of nationalism, which
continues to deprive the world's peoples of a genuine sense of humanity as a whole. In the Church, ignorance about the role of the
layman in the Church and the deplorable lack of a Christian social
awareness among Church members take a much higher place as
serious problems. Would that Pope Paul's "On the Development of
Peoples" had aroused as much discussion, dispute, and action! There
exists a radical dislocation in the Christian consciousness when a
question which centers on self brings more concern and reaction
than one which centers on others.

Reactions of Individuals

How can we characterize individuals' reactions to the encyclical
"Concerning Human Life"? They have been ordinary in one sense
—that reactions to commandment, law, directives always fall into
one of three categories, two making the legislation useless and one
making it useful. The range of reactions is the same, whether it
pertains to Moses on Sinai proclaiming, "Thou shalt not kill," a
parent requiring his child to be back by midnight on his night out,
or a civil official forbidding the public to litter the roadside with
trash.

Regulation is useless for one section of the constituency, those
who, even before the law was promulgated, hadn't the slightest
intention of doing what the law opposes. Had Moses never said,
"Thou shalt not kill," faithful Levi would never have murdered
anybody in his life. Had his father not insisted, good son John
would have been home by midnight anyway. Had the antilitter

sign never been put up every thousand yards along the road, Mr. Wheeler would still not have cluttered up the landscape. The other kind of person for whom the law is useless is the one who will disregard its stipulations, whatever the consequences. A man like this who intended to murder someone would not have changed his mind in the least after hearing Moses' injunction. Penalty or no penalty, bad son Jim will come back from his date whenever he pleases, and Mr. Driver will litter the roadside to his heart's content. On the other hand, the people who will find regulations useful are those who want and need guidance—the uninstructed, the imperfect, the weak. These would not have known how to act or might have moved toward error had the law not been promulgated to inform them.

Considering the encyclical in these terms provides a more balanced view of the reactions it has evoked. It has instructed and confirmed the good will and actions of some. It has become a sign of contradiction to others. And it has fulfilled its purpose by giving guidance to those who needed it and will respond to the best of their ability.

One reaction appears as a gross misunderstanding: that the Pope is against birth control. The right of married couples to decide how many children to have and when to have them is uncontested. This encyclical concerns the morality of means taken toward that end. Other reactions are legalistic and pharisaic. Legal purists would make sure they followed the letter of the law but would discount the fact that purpose and circumstances also affect the morality of an act. In this way, some would consider themselves "safe" (legalism's motto is "Safety first!") if they scrupulously used the rhythm method, though their motivation might be totally selfish. Pharisaism would infect those who presumed to condemn others who did not conform to the prescriptions of the encyclical; there are times when we have to judge others lest we attribute good fruit to a bad tree, but no one has the right to condemn another in this matter.

Some react wrongly by default. These consider that the subject matter of the encyclical doesn't concern them because they are not involved in it owing to their circumstances. The unmarried, those who cannot have children though married, the very old, the very young can dismiss the issue as not their affair. They can even feel glad that what bothers so many others doesn't bother them. This is a strain of individualism which contradicts charity; what is of vital importance for any members of the Church is of vital importance for all. No single cell in the body can ignore the health of the rest of the body.

Some well-formulated objections to the encyclical "Concerning Human Life," based on intellectual rather than psychological or emotional reactions, disagree with Pope Paul's arguments for his position. The misery and suffering which exist in certain parts of the world because of overpopulation are most cogent reasons for birth control. But the Pope insists that only rightful moral means be used to assuage this distressing situation. The people of the world have ample resources to help all if they would distribute the world's goods equitably. Social injustice is more the root of the problem than overpopulation. Government propaganda often presents artificial birth control as if it were the only answer because it seems to be the cheapest and quickest solution. Readjusting world trade and aid, raising the age of marriage, broadcasting more efficient agricultural methods, working generously with the United Nations are answers one hardly ever hears about.

Separating human sexuality from its life-producing effect seems to be justified by some with the argument that the satisfaction of the need for love and affection through intercourse is an essential purpose of marriage. This is not denied in the encyclical. Indeed, the recognition of this fact in the documents of Vatican II was a major advance over the inadequate perceptions of the past. However, does the realization of one essential end in marriage justify a deliberate attempt to exclude the realization of another, that of child-bearing? Must not both ends be fully respected? Each is as sacred as the other.

The Pope's appeal to the natural law is contested on the ground that the traditional understanding of natural law is obsolete. Some moderns see a new natural law governing the new man of today. John Courtney Murray has characterized this view as "the new rationalism." [1] It grants man an autonomy over the rest of nature in the sense that he transcends it. It abandons the deductive argumentation of the old view in favor of total patterns, the "so-called principle of totality" mentioned in section 3 of the encyclical. [2] The natural law is identified with the drive of the whole personality, "the totality of the impulses whereby men strive to live ever more fully." [3] Nature and its laws are no longer to be considered static; the new view "supplements the processes of reason with the proc-

[1] John Courtney Murray, *We Hold These Truths*, Garden City, N.Y., Doubleday & Company, Image Book, 1964, p. 305.
[2] *"Humanae vitae* (Human Life)," *Catholic Mind,* September, 1968, p. 36.
[3] Murray, *loc. cit.*

esses of history and the consequent experience of change and evolution." [4] Nature evolves and natural law emerges. However, the concept of natural law employed by Pope Paul stands firmly on metaphysical foundations; it is as valid today as it ever was in the past
and will be in the future. John Courtney Murray characterizes it
very positively and solidly:

> The whole metaphysic involved in the idea of the natural law
> may seem alarmingly complicated; in a sense it is. Natural law
> supposes a realist epistemology, [which] asserts the real to be the
> measure of knowledge, and also asserts the possibility of intelligence
> reaching the real, *i.e.*, the nature of things—in this case, the nature
> of man as a unitary and constant concept beneath all individual
> differences. Secondly, it supposes a metaphysic of nature, especially
> the idea that nature is a teleological concept, that the "form" of a
> thing is its "final cause," the goal of its becoming; in this case, that
> there is a natural inclination in man to become what in nature and
> destination he is—to achieve the fullness of his own being. Thirdly,
> it supposes a natural theology, asserting that there is a God Who
> is eternal Reason, *Nous*, at the summit of the order of being, Who
> is the author of all nature, and Who wills that the order of nature
> be fulfilled in all its purposes, as these are inherent in the natures
> found in that order. Finally, it supposes a morality, especially the
> principle that for man, a rational being, the order of nature is not
> an order of necessity, to be fulfilled blindly, but an order of reason
> and therefore of freedom. The order of being that confronts his
> intelligence is an order of "oughtness" for his will; the moral order
> is a prolongation of the metaphysical order into the dimension of
> human freedom.[5]

Reactions of Theologians

What of the reactions of the qualified theologian to the encyclical
"Concerning Human Life"? Precisely because of his qualifications,
it is his task to subject the encyclical to critical evaluation and explanation. He must operate as the professional scientist that he is. If
he finds that the Pope's reasons for his conclusions lack persuasive-
ness, he must say so, if simply for the sake of intellectual honesty. If
he can only adjudge after careful and thorough study that the Pope
has failed to take into sufficient consideration factors derived from
the subsidiary sciences of psychology, demography, sociology, or
any other pertinent field, he must air and discuss his thoughts with
his scientific peers, fulfilling the important function he has in the
Church of contributing to a deeper understanding of truth.

[4] *Ibid.*
[5] *Ibid.*, p. 310.

The hazards of the theologian here are great, in accordance with the great responsibility which is his. He can succeed admirably in the performance of his science but fail miserably in other ways, as in regard to prudence. For example, the following statement from the original eighty-seven dissenting theologians in Washington, D.C., is correct:

> It is common teaching in the Church that Catholics may dissent from authoritative, noninfallible teachings of the magisterium when sufficient reasons for so doing exist.

However, the paragraph which follows oversteps the bounds of prudence in this very important matter:

> Therefore, as Roman Catholic theologians, conscious of our duty and our limitations, we conclude that spouses may responsibly decide according to their conscience that artificial contraception in some circumstances is permissible and indeed necessary to preserve and foster the values and sacredness of marriage.[6]

The presumption in the pastoral advice is this: because we as theologians disagree with the Pope's reasons for his stand, as outlined in our statement, we have the right, even the duty to advise the faithful that they can opt noncompliance for their own reasons. It seems to say that the Pope's authority is binding only to the extent that we agree with his reasons, that his authority is only as good as his reasons. If this is so, then analogically, a teen-ager does not owe obedience to his parents if he disagrees with their reasons for their commands; especially may he refuse obedience if he knows for sure their reasons are illogical, unfounded, or contradicted by scientists. This posture is strongly antagonistic to the position of the German theologian Karl Rahner, who maintains:

> An opinion which opposes the temporary ecclesiastical doctrinal expression in any instance does not belong in preaching and in catechetics, even if the faithful under these circumstances are to be educated about the essence and the limited significance of such a temporary doctrinal decision. . . . Whoever thinks that he is permitted to have his own private opinion and that in this he has a better future insight than the church must ask himself before God and his conscience, in a reasonable self-critical evaluation, whether he has the necessary breadth and depth of factual theological knowledge to be permitted to depart in his private theories and practice from the present doctrine of the official church. Such a case is basically conceivable. But subjective arrogance and smart-

[6] "Washington, D.C., Theologians," *Catholic Mind*, September, 1968, p. 3.

aleckness will have to answer for [themselves] before the judgment of God.[7]

The theologian's difficulty is compounded if he is a priest. As both a member of that community which is the Church and the Church's official representative in the confessional, to what degree if any may he give advice contradictory to the instruction of the encyclical? Also, a priest's powers are delegated powers, delegated to him by his bishop; he neither has nor exercises his powers in his own right. If he feels he cannot in conscience advise according to official papal pronouncements, does integrity demand that he ask to be relieved of those offices wherein he would be obliged to treat of the matter of the encyclical by counsel, preaching, or teaching? How absolute are his right and duty to proclaim the truth as he sees it?

Heresy is the occupational hazard of the theologian. It takes a theologian to be a heretic; anybody else would generally be excused on the grounds of ignorance. The theologian *should* know better. Were a theologian to go beyond a critique of the arguments and conclusions of the encyclical, to the point of challenging the *authority* involved, he would thereby undermine his own position. As a matter of fact, he cannot challenge the authority of the encyclical *as a theologian*. He may do so as a historian, a philosopher, a sociologist, or simply as a man, but he cannot do so qua theologian.

No scientist is allowed as scientist to challenge the main premise of his science. He investigates, searches, thinks, concludes, enunciates, implicitly taking his first principles and main premise for granted. A physicist assumes the existence of matter and quantity as given. The moment he brings the existence of physical matter into question, he becomes a philosopher and is no longer a physicist; he cannot make this challenge qua physicist. The theologian receives his premises by way of authority, and his science consists in what he does with these premises from that point onward. The moment he challenges the authority, he destroys his own science.

If a theologian steadfastly holds to a conclusion which he bases on the deposit of faith in the face of the Church's determination that his conclusion is erroneous, then he becomes a heretic, a theologian who is obstinately wrong. But he is still a theologian. If he goes to the extent of challenging the authority itself which gives

[7] "Rahner on the Encyclical *Humanae vitae*," *National Catholic Reporter*, September 18, 1968, p. 7.

him his premises, he pulls the rug out from under his own feet. He destroys himself as a theologian. The science of theology is not absolute; it derives from and depends upon the magisterium, which is in no way necessarily dependent upon it. Much confusion among lay people on this and other matters would dissipate if they would distinguish precisely between what is Church teaching and what is theological speculation. These are two very different things. Theology's contributions to religious well-being are rich and nourishing; yet the Gospel, the Church, the magisterium could survive, if not so well, without theological speculation.

The theologian must also respect the principle of subordination in the hierarchy of the sciences. While in his search for truth he must explicate what is implicitly contained in the teachings of faith, using knowledge obtained from all relevant sources and disciplines in the process, it is his further and equally important responsibility to put that truth in proper perspective. The sociological answer to a problem may not be at that moment the moral answer. A conclusion verified in experimental psychology may have to be profoundly modified by the metaphysics of man. A doctor's decision to perform an abortion may be the medical answer required in a situation, it may be the sociological answer and also the psychological one, but it may not be the human answer or the moral one. The best military retort to an approaching battle may have to be radically qualified or even entirely overruled by the political necessities of international affairs.

Morality as a science must have recourse to the science of sociology for information necessary to make true moral judgments. But sociological truths do not *replace* moral truths; they supply morality with that certain knowledge which it needs for the progressive understanding, development, and restatement of moral truths. In "Concerning Human Life," Pope Paul implies that no sociological or other data exist as yet to justify any modification of the traditional papal moral teaching on artificial birth control. But he acknowledges that data may become available in the future from the advance of the sciences and human experience which will require or enable the Church to change its present moral position. Today, the theologian would serve the cause of truth much better if, instead of using conclusions from subordinate sciences to contradict the moral position of the encyclical, they encouraged and helped the development of those sciences of humanity whose conclusions can add new data for further moral consideration.

In the matter of giving truth from whatever source its proper place, there arises the problem of the sources of truth within the Church. There are theologians who seem to maintain that the Pope's position in "Concerning Human Life" is inadequate or does not represent fully the truth of the Holy Spirit because a *collegium* of the bishops or the collective sentiment of the faithful, the people of God, might view the matter differently. Such an argument ignores the primacy of the Pope's position in the Church. One may demand that the Pope consult these other sources of expression of truth in the Church; it might be very imprudent for him not to. But the demand cannot imply that because he freely chose not to, his conclusions do not belong to his magisterial power or lack a certain fullness of truth which they must have. That the Spirit of God speaks and directs the Church through the *collegium* of bishops and the people of God as a whole neither modifies nor cancels the fact that He speaks through the Pope also, and can speak through the Pope alone.

While proclaiming rightly the primacy of conscience as the first principle of morality, the theologian must take care that conscience is understood properly and that, as the prime internal principle of all morality, it is related to law, which is the external and objective principle of morality. Too often people talk of their consciences when what they are referring to is merely their feelings. People who answer inquiries on polls or questionnaires on points of conscience are frequently recording only their first unreflective reactions, the effect a question has on the superficial, unexamined level of their sensibilities, a level which of itself does not yield objective truth. In his judgment of conscience, the Catholic Christian includes, among necessarily pertinent elements, what the teaching of the Church is on a matter; he does not use his conscience to judge the Church, nor does he use it separately from the Church.

The theologian, scientist that he is, recognizes the fact that there is no science of the particular. A science consists in principles to be employed in judgments concerning particular cases. The scientist of morality does not start his thinking from the viewpoint of the way-out case and attempt to determine from its circumstances what the moral standard should be. In teaching, for example, he begins with a statement and explanation of the basic principles involved in a particular case before he begins to apply them to it. In the formulation of a principle, account cannot be taken of all the possible circumstances which can modify the answer to any particular problem. The theologian cannot work backward and use circumstances to cancel out principles. "To diminish in no way the saving teaching of Christ constitutes an eminent form of charity for souls," [8] the Pope states in the encyclical. However, in employing his science as a theologian and in advising as confessor or counselor, the priest has room for infinite understanding and compassion.

Indeed, the great merit of "Concerning Human Life" may not be that men clearly comprehend and agree with its reasonings and its statements, nor even that they find conformity with its ideal possible in the world of today, but rather that in their difficulties in this regard the faithful hear, beyond strife, beyond confusion, in their pastors and in their priests, "the echo of the voice and love of the Redeemer." [9]

[8] *"Humanae vitae* (Human Life)," p. 46.
[9] *Ibid.*

REV. THOMAS A. WASSMER, S.J.

10 Contemporary Situational
Morality and the Catholic Christian

There is little doubt that in Catholic colleges, the teaching of ethics has undergone enormous changes in the last several years. This is certainly due to the metamorphoses elsewhere in our culture. Students coming into the study of philosophy and learning for the first time the speculative sides of questions that they have already been experiencing in their lives for some years are stubbornly resisting any presentation that proceeds deductively from an examination of rational human nature regarded as a universal essence.

In other words, students of ethics are aware of the contemporary intellectual mind, and find themselves more and more sympathetic with the way it operates. This mental set has been described as exhibiting four major characteristics: (1) a sense of historical evolution, (2) an awareness of subjectivity growing out of developments in contemporary psychology, (3) a science-inspired suspicion of any position that is not empirically verifiable, and (4) an appreciation of the human situation as described in existential theology and existential phenomenology. These four characteristics seriously confront the ethician lecturing to a college class, and he must be aware of the roles they play in his students' thinking and acting. It is futile for him to propose an ethic that is only a plausible theory and not operational in their own lives. In fact, it is idle to propose an ethic that is not operational in his own.

The great challenge for the ethician is to show that his conclusions are not alien to the scientific attitude and that they can in some way be empirically verified. Most students are attracted by intrinsic values, but often question whether they are so patent or demonstrable. Is it possible for a student to subscribe to absolutized honesty or fidelity, for instance, when he is convinced that in the present existential situation it is destructive of certain other values with which it is in conflict? Values in themselves are easily appreciated and admired. But when they are found in a constellation of competing elements, the student begins asking embarrassing questions about which should survive in the encounter, including the very values which have been identified with the Catholic. Currently, for example, direct killing and sexuality are being subjected to re-examination by some moralists in something of a situational context.

The Ethic of Responsibility
and the Ethic of Conviction

Anyone who attempts to propose a relevant and significant ethic today must take into account the type of ethical thinking that is going on. It is found in many Protestant and Catholic groups, and the students are experiencing it although they may be hearing a different kind of ethical analysis in the lecture halls. For this reason, efforts have to be made to bring together in living contact the best features of situational morality with the traditional morality of the past.

Perhaps the best way to begin this development of a contemporary ethic is to state and defend a few propositions of my own. It seems to me that the authentic morality is one resulting from the dialectical tension of two ethics, the *ethic of responsibility* and the *ethic of conviction*. Let me explain the root meaning of both terms. The ethic of responsibility is one whose ultimate concern is personal consequences, the empirical, verifiable results that eventuate from an act. It is in terms of these consequences that the act is characterized as good or bad. On the other hand, the ethic of conviction is one whose ultimate concern is principle, and it is more or less indifferent to consequences. Situational morality tends to polarize and absolutize the first ethic and traditional morality the second. The past has been more interested in the ethic of conviction; the present thinking is more in the direction of an ethic of responsibility.

My position is that a person cannot consistently live by either ethic but must live by both, in dynamic dialectical tension. Nevertheless, much of the criticism of leaders in civil society or in the Church is raised by persons who use only one of these ethics as the norm for their judgments. Let me illustrate.

Rolf Hochhuth, in his play *The Deputy*, censures Pope Pius XII for not having spoken out against the Nazis because, the playwright seems to think, the Holy Father should have been obligated primarily if not solely by an ethic of conviction. Even if the worst results would have befallen the Christian churches, the voice of the Holy Father should never have remained silent. He should not have calculated the consequences; others may do this, but not a pope. The pope, in other words, should be a man of principle, directed by the ethic of conviction and not by the ethic of responsibility. Is this reasonable or unreasonable? To live by one ethic rather than by both in dynamic tension strikes me as most unreasonable and unrealistic.

An example may be given of a form of criticism which implies that the object criticized should be directed primarily if not uniquely by an ethic of responsibility. Numerous Catholic journals have been sharp with Paul VI because, they say, his pronouncement on contraception neglects the personal empirical consequences, disruptive of marital harmony, that result if rhythm is the sole means allowed for practicing responsible parenthood. On the other hand, it is argued, the empirically verifiable consequences of contraception work to the harmony of marriage and to the mutual personal satisfaction of the couple. The principle in this mode of argument is that the Pope was obligated to recognize the good consequences that follow from the practice of contraception. Implicit in all this is that the ethic of responsibility should have exercised priority here. Once again, the criticism proceeds from the adoption of one polar ethical position rather than the recognition that the Pope found himself in the ambiguous position of trying to reconcile the two ethics of responsibility and conviction.

A final illustration can be taken from an experience which is most contemporaneous: the case of the conscientious objector who is opposed to a particular war, such as that in Vietnam. Specific conscientious objection status is not recognized at present by the law; therefore, faced with a conflict between his conscience and military service laws, the individual has two basic alternatives. He can be directed by the ethic of conviction and accept the consequences, which will probably be painful to him. These consequences are primarily ones that befall *him*, not others. Or he can be directed by both ethics and thus also experience the ethic of responsibility in his moral choice. The latter course brings into view the empirically verifiable effects upon others, both fellow nonparticipants and participants. For the ethic of responsibility opens a person to all the consequences, to others as well as himself; without it, the ethic of conviction can be a cold and mindless thing. The ethic of conviction is the encounter of a person with law, while the ethic of responsibility is the encounter of a person with the Person who is incarnate in all other persons.

Just consider how difficult the situation becomes for the man who is struggling to be more and more responsible. Instead of immediately deciding on conviction that he should not enter a war, he proceeds to re-examine the notion of participation in a war and wartime practices that he considers unjust, illegal, and immoral. If he looks to the Nuremberg precedent for guidance, it seems to me that he will *not* take the view that *any* participation in the armed forces is necessarily immoral, any more than it is criminal under international law. If he participates, as marginally as possible, and manages with good fortune to stay out of positions and situations where immoral behavior is almost unavoidable, I would think that he has not necessarily betrayed his conscience. After all, if people did not ethicize in this way, they could never have German friends who served in the German armed forces during the Second World War in even a remote and marginal capacity.

No one questions that these difficult situational decisions should be left exclusively to the individual. Criticism can be made, however, of the man who thinks that he is more ethical if he is guided only by conviction. "The man for all seasons," Saint Thomas More, was quite the calculator; in fact, most of his life seemed to be controlled by the ethic of responsibility. The empirically verifiable consequences to his family, his country, himself—he had no taste for death—were most operational in this thinking. Only toward the very end did the resolution of the tension become manifest, when principle and conviction were in deadly combat with these consequences.

Let us apply some of this tension to the painful decision that the young man must make who is convinced of the unethical and immoral nature of a specific war or war practice. As he contemplates these difficult situational decisions, I would suggest, he might re-examine the idea that as war service necessarily means a sharing of all the moral consequences that flow from the character of the war, refusal to serve effectively means *nonparticipation*. Then where does this nonparticipation stop? If the conscientious objector is really serious, he might ponder the writings of Walter Stein and his English Catholic pacifist colleagues. Perhaps nonparticipation should take the form of boycotting political elections. For some it may consist in refusing to pay taxes. But what about the universities that are carrying out government-supported research, and what about government-subsidized scholarships and loans? Is a draftee who folds blankets for a year in a supply room at Fort Dix participating in an unjust war to a decisively greater degree than a student attending a university heavily subsidized by federal funds? *Is nonparticipation mainly a question of uniform?*

The more responsible the individual, the more is he aware of all the consequences involved, not only in participation but also in nonparticipation. In the case of conscientious objection to a war, he is bound to ask eventually, where shall our nonparticipation stop? Here we have come to the real existential agony of the whole problem of evil and how we contribute to it. Unavoidably, ineluctably, we do contribute to the quantity of evil in the world. What does this ulti-mately mean? A French film of recent years had as its theme the notion that possibly we should measure the success of our lives by the amount of evil we have been able to avoid rather than only by the quantity of good we have done. If there is ambiguity in the moral decision made by attempting to reconcile the two ethics of responsibility and conviction, it is only because we are in a world of enormous good and enormous evil.

It is foolish for us to deny that in the ambivalence of our own moral and ethical lives, we are contributing to one another's unin-tended delinquency. While we pride ourselves on our rational ex-istence—in which nonetheless so much rationalization is present—we should not overlook this truth. It is in the light of this ambivalence that we should approach the most profound and painful decisions regarding participation in what we are convinced is evil: decisions on the proximity of the evil and the avoidability of the participa-tion, decisions on our freedom and the limitations on it in a wounded society of man. It is only in this light that the responsibility as well as the conviction of the person will grow. In other words, it is only by experiencing the ambiguity of moral decisions that we will come to an appreciation of a genuine ethic, one which will be personal, autonomous, and authentic.

This, then, is the first proposition that appears to me to be theo-retically and practically defensible: a person cannot live constantly and uniformly by just one of these two ethics; he must live by both in dynamic dialectical tension.

Let me now advance to my second proposition.

In the ethic of responsibility, empirically verifiable evidence is of great importance, and is sought to demonstrate the value in the existential moral act here and now. The empirical data may not bear out the universal affirmative principles and negative prohibitions that we have associated with the ethic of conviction. Nevertheless, this evidence is called for more and more in the methodological and systematic presentation of any contemporary and meaningful ethic. The moral absolutes that we associate with the ethic of conviction should be supported by the empirical evidence.

As I have pointed out, students are increasingly asking why the values implicit in the moral absolutes appear more and more to be deprived of evidence in any conflict with other values. Does the empirically verifiable evidence support contraception or rhythm? Does it corroborate the arguments for the absolute indissolubility of marriage? Does it reinforce the absolutist position vis-à-vis the value of physical life?

Only in the order of sexuality and direct killing does the ethic of conviction for the Catholic moralist seem to be still standing. But has some erosion taken place even among these moral imperatives? Even here, is the concept of intrinsic evil viable any more, or do so many adjuncts have to be added to the original moral object that the notion no longer is useful in moral discourse?

I will attempt to show that the idea of intrinsic evil applied to a particular act is not viable as a term in moral discourse, and that it can operate as an albatross around the neck of the user. It seems to me that this has happened in the treatment of contraception, and that now the harsh moral term remains one of the principal difficulties in the current discussions among moralists. A moral act can still be designated as wrong without bringing out megaton phrases like "intrinsic evil" and "evil of its very nature."

It is hard for anyone to see how a given marital practice can be intrinsically evil which is not supported by the empirically verifiable data in the largest number of ethical and moral married unions. Shortly before this writing, a Jesuit journal discussed the difficulties that many couples were finding with the practice of rhythm, and commented that this seemed to indicate the necessity of some form of contraception for marital harmony and happiness. Does this not seem to be stating that the empirical evidence behind rhythm is open to question and that the data appear to be in favor of contraception? If these points are true, then the prohibition of contraception is no longer supported by the findings in the largest number of marriages. In other words, the ethic of conviction regarding contraception is unsubstantiated by the evidence which people are seeking in their moral experience. People are increasingly seeking an ethic that will be reasonable. The pendulum is swinging more and more toward an ethic of responsibility and away from convictions that are not borne out by empirical data.

To say this is not to claim for the evidence that it necessarily constitutes the ethical or moral nature of the act, though it does manifest that nature in some way. It surely seems strange to the unsophisticated in moral science that affirmative and negative moral principles are maintained in the face of contradictory evidence. This evidence thus requires the constant attention of the moral philosopher; he cannot ignore it and insist that his thinking is relevant and contemporary. For the person of faith, accepting the prohibitions against divorce, abortion, and contraception may not occasion the agonies they do for the person without the faith. Nevertheless, even the believer finds the difficulties mounting when he is told that his faith is eminently reasonable, that "faith builds upon reason," and then discovers that the empirically verifiable evidence does not bear out its moral absolutes.

To me, the few moral absolutes that do remain in the ethic of conviction are in the order of sexuality and direct killing. Yet one wonders, as I have said, whether even these are any longer validated by sufficient empirically verifiable evidence. For example, do the knowns in favor of contraception in the present historical context outweigh those against it? Therefore, does it seem wise to designate contraception as intrinsically evil, evil *semper et pro semper?* Is it wise to make contraception a prescriptive principle? Any imperative, moral or positive, should be first an *ordinance of reason for the common good.* Does this not seem to indicate that its reasonableness should become manifest in the empirically verifiable ethical and moral living of persons?

I should make clear that my dissatisfaction is not with characterizing contraception, direct killing, and divorce as unethical under most circumstances. My complaint is against qualifying these moral acts as *intrinsically* wrong in the face of contradictory findings. What I am saying reductively is that while noncontraceptive relations and absolutely indissoluble marriages might be the ideal, *is the ideal always a moral imperative?* Are we wise in insisting that moral disvalues are always forbidden, and that in the concrete situation they are always unethical and morally wrong to bring about? In two articles of mine, I attempted to show that the notion of intrinsic evil is not operational in contemporary ethical discourse.[1] Father

Milhaven has complemented these efforts by demonstrating how we can know which values are absolute. Bishop Simons[2] and Dennis Doherty[3] continue Milhaven's and my speculation by applying these norms to such practices as masturbation and premarital intercourse, and ultimately admit that these should not be designated as intrinsically evil. No one of the four moralists would question the unethical nature of these acts. They are rather pinpointing the crucial issues of just how these values are vindicated and supported, and whether the ideal situation should always be a moral imperative. It is situational morality that has brought about much of this re-examination.

Let me summarize, then, the second proposition in the light of everything that has been said to develop it in the last few pages. The ethic of conviction turns principally on moral absolutes regarding sexuality and direct killing. With the speculation that has been focused on these two subjects, it can be asked whether they are any longer moral absolutes in the sense of being validated by sufficient empirically verifiable data. If they are not, and it seems to me that they are not, is it wise to characterize these acts any longer as intrinsically evil? The question can be posed in another form: if these areas can no longer be classified as intrinsically good and necessary to preserve at any ethical cost; and if contraception, direct killing, and divorce in the case of a sacramental and consummated marriage are no longer to be defined as intrinsically wrong, then might we not admit that there is some validity in saying that an erosion has taken hold in the last few moral absolutes? Is it reasonable to call them moral absolutes when the data are no longer supporting them? Is this not what Bishop Simons, Doherty, Milhaven, and Wassmer seem to be saying? Is it so temerarious to suggest that the moral situation questions the validity of universal affirmative principles and especially of universal negative prohibitions?

Let me now consider the third proposition in the structuring of a contemporary relevant moral philosophy. It might be put this way: every value (life, promise-keeping, fidelity, whatever) should be seen never in isolation but in a constellation of other values and dis-

[1] Thomas A. Wassmer, S.J., "Morality and Intrinsic Evil," *Catholic Lawyer*, II (1965), 180–183, and "Is Intrinsic Evil a Viable Term?", *Chicago Studies*, V (1966), 307–314.

[2] Bishop Francis Simons, "The Catholic Church and the New Morality," *Cross Currents*, XVI (Fall, 1966), 429–445.

[3] Dennis Doherty, "Sexual Morality: Absolute or Situational?", *Continuum*, V, no. 2 (Summer, 1967), 235–253.

values; none should be so polarized or absolutized that it is viewed essentially and not existentially in concrete phenomenological experience. For each is surrounded by a multiplicity of other values and disvalues which have to be harmonized and synthesized into a reasonable ethical gestalt. No one doubts that a resolute stand in favor of the value of physical life, procreation, or the absolute indissolubility of marriage, for example, is admirable and often defensible. However, it is justifiable to question whether polarizing and absolutizing one such value is realistic when in the human situation it is always found in a vortex of values and disvalues which have to be experienced and resolved. For example, is it always reasonable to respect the physical life of the embryo (doubtfully rational at the moment of conception) at the expense of the quality of life or the mother? Is there not some inconsistency between superlative concern for intrauterine physical life and indifference to the quality of its existence in countries suffering visibly from population problems?

Life would be simple and uncomplicated if only one value had to be protected, but this is never the case. Values compete with one another in the human situation, and existential experience is never the mere observation of intrinsic good and intrinsic evil. Other values press in on ethical circumstances; disvalues assert themselves and narrow the area of the moral. The contextual analysis of any moral situation in business or medicine will make it obvious that moral imperatives must wait in the wings until all the values and disvalues are heard.

Responsibility is not the immediate application of a single universal affirmative or negative principle. It is the slow, torturous, prismatic analysis which softens the affirmative command and alters the negative prescription. Entering into a contextual discussion of a moral case with persons of different ethical backgrounds, one must listen quietly to all the voices and claims that arise, all the values and disvalues that are seen more by others than ourselves, and then offer humbly, tentatively, hesitantly, stammeringly the final resolution of the conflicting claims on conscience. Such an experience will educate the most naive. It may lead to longer examinations of conscience and to longer professional relationships with a confessor. It certainly will generate respect for the depth of every conscience, for the intrinsic worth of every person.

It is not extraordinary that this period of our history is characterized by a refined conception of the person and a real appreciation of the inviolability of conscience. If the person has dignity, it is because of his conscience. It is in conscience that one person meets the Person, and before him resolves all the claims set up by the values and disvalues that operate with himself in the center of the vortex. Conscience is not a person before the law; it is a person before the Person, and before him he makes the prismatic analysis of the conflict of values and disvalues. It is here where real responsibility is manifest, and where existential experience produces maturity and real growth. It is a paradox but true that the harder ethic to live is the ethic of responsibility and not the ethic of conviction. Hardest of all is to live by both ethics in dialectical tension and to resolve personally the claims and counterclaims that arise from all the values and disvalues in the moral experience. It is the hardest morality of all, but it is the only morality that will be true to the metaphysics of conscience.

The Importance of Evidence for Contemporary Ethics

In order to clarify the precise difference between the two ethics and to aid in the resolution of the tension between them, let us consider the importance of the role of empirically verifiable data. Traditional morality, which places so much emphasis upon the ethic of conviction, argues that no amount of evidence can invalidate absolute intrinsic values. Any evidence which can be brought to bear in favor of the intrinsic value is something additional; any evidence adduced from consequences to show the wrongness of an intrinsic evil will only be an extrinsic argument against the really intrinsic wrongness.

In other words, evidence plays a minor role if any in the ethic of conviction. Circumstances or other evidence will possibly be employed to show that there are great difficulties in applying the ethic of conviction immediately, that the responsibility of the person is reduced, and that the place of prudence in the matter is highly important. Nevertheless, empirical evidence is extrinsic to the consideration of absolute values. By its very definition, the notion of intrinsic value arises from a relationship with the idea of rational human nature looked at adequately. Conversely, intrinsic evil is predicated of an act which, when one prescinds from motive and circumstances, is always in disagreement with rational human nature looked at adequately.

It must be apparent that the notions of intrinsic good and evil are philosophically wedded to an essentialistic consideration of human nature. Evidence in such a systematic presentation plays an *epistemological* role but never the *ontological* role of structuring the very values or disvalues themselves. It is here that the issue between the ethic of responsibility and the ethic of conviction is really placed. For the ethic of responsibility, evidence plays both an ontological and an epistemological role. The empirically verifiable data not only *show* but *constitute* the rightness or wrongness of an act. We can see why these two ethics are in a dialectical tension that enters into their resolution in a genuine decision of conscience. These considerations throw a fundamental question into sharpest relief: is empirically verifiable evidence to play merely an epistemological role, of making the quality of the moral act manifest, or is it to play in addition an ontological role, constituting the very structure of the moral act?

My own thinking at present is the result of several papers on the nonviability of the concept of intrinsic evil. Proceeding from the admitted paucity of acts which are intrinsically evil, we can draw the tentative conclusion that we must re-evaluate the role of evidence more and more, for empirical data seem to be required not only for epistemological purposes but for ontological ones as well. In other words, at the present historical moment, the ethic of responsibility is assuming greater importance in a genuine ethic.

In an article in *Commonweal*,[4] Daniel Callahan placed his finger on the nerve ends of the two ethics in their attitude toward the importance of the empirical data. For example, one who considers the practice of divorce to be morally wrong and never permitted will argue that in the generality of cases, divorce is socially harmful —in other words, that the moral absolute against divorce is supported by the empirical data. Nevertheless, the evidence is hardly so decisive as to establish its necessary evil in every case. As a matter of fact, almost everyone can find within his own circle of friends or relatives instances where divorce and remarriage seem to have promoted some notable social goods (children restored to normal life, an end to parental fighting, and so on). As the generality of cases is sufficient for the moral philosopher who defends the ethic of conviction with its notion of intrinsic good and evil, this raises some very interesting questions about the interplay of evidence and the ethic of conviction. If a moral absolute was not borne out by the

[4] Daniel Callahan, "Ethics and Evidence," *Commonweal*, October 21, 1966, pp. 76–78.

evidence in the generality of cases, would the ethic of conviction undergo a change on the notion of intrinsic value? To illustrate, suppose it could be shown that in the generality of successful marriages, the empirical evidence was in favor of the adoption of contraception as opposed to the practice of rhythm: would the ethicist who has held to the intrinsic disvalue of contraception allow his position to undergo a change? It is conceivable at least that the findings would be in favor of the change in what was originally a moral absolute. Would it then have to yield as an absolute?

There are additional problems for anyone who takes the empirical data seriously. Ethicists who accept the generality of cases as sufficient to show that the moral absolute has been vindicated by the evidence adjudge that these counterbalance the exceptional cases which do not provide support. But does this attitude grant due importance to the role of evidence? Where there is almost a parity of evidence for and against the moral absolute, is the ethicist willing to "tailor" (the word is Callahan's) the principle in order to give full play to the range of findings? If so, the moral absolute would forbid a practice like divorce where the empirical data show that it would probably be harmful to individuals and society and allow it where only slight evil or none would result. Callahan does not think that the moralist is really considering the evidence with great seriousness if he is unwilling to adapt his moral principles in this way.

When the issue is expressed in these terms, the nerve ends of the ethicist are exposed. What are his presuppositions? In choosing between the two ethics, one where evidence plays an ontological, structuring part and the other where it operates only epistemologically, which takes priority with the ethicist? If my own position is valid, that a man must live by both in real dialectical tension, then repeated and anguished ambivalence is the lot of every man, and no one will know the outcome but God and the individual conscience.

Callahan and others have shown how James Gustafson of the Yale Department of Religious Studies has helped explain the nature of moral precepts with his plausible distinction between a "prescriptive" and an "illuminative" use of principles.[5] In the first, "The center of gravity is on the reliability of traditional moral propositions." They are considered to be the "most important or sole authority for the governing of action." In the second, the principles are used "to *interpret* what is morally wrong and morally right

---

[5] James Gustafson, "Context Versus Principles: A Misplaced Debate in Christian Ethics," in Marty Peerman, ed., *New Theology*, no. 3, New York, The Macmillan Company, 1966, p. 70.

about a particular occasion." The center of gravity here is on "the newness, the openness, the freedom that is present. . . ." With this distinction, Gustafson contends that the discussion over context versus principles is "misplaced": according to him, it is a question not of ethicists' choosing one or the other but of the use they assign to principles. This appears to be in agreement with my own position, that the evidence for some values will have at most an epistemological bearing while for others, much more contextual, it will play in addition an ontological role. It appears to me that ethicists are increasingly giving the evidence the center of gravity and expecting the principle to be open to corrigibility if the findings are against it.

Gustafson's contributions to this general discussion are now accepted by almost all moralists. He shows how contemporary ethicists usually begin from one of four places: (1) some start with "as accurate and perceptive a social or situational analysis as possible"; (2) some "begin with fundamental theological affirmations"; (3) "still others locate moral principles as the center point for discussion"; (4) and some, finally, depart from "the nature of the Christian's life in Christ and its proper expression in moral conduct." Regardless of where the ethicist sets out from, the direction is always toward a consideration of the relationship of that starting point to the other three. If numbers 2 and 4 are considered with real seriousness, we will have to say that the role of evidence will be assuming more and more importance in ethical discussions and that moral absolutes will have to be re-evaluated again and again.

At the opening of this chapter, I outlined four characteristics of the contemporary intellectual mind, one of which was a suspicion of any position not empirically verifiable. This attitude is increasingly found with regard to moral positions that need to be considered seriously by contemporary man. Empirical findings have had an enormous impact upon the modern Catholic consciousness. Witness the role they are playing in the justified arguments for a change in Church attitudes toward contraception. As Callahan has remarked in *Commonweal:*

> Whether moralists like it or not, Catholics today are influenced by empirical evidence and by their own experience. The sudden collapse of opposition in many quarters to the use of contraceptives reflects the impact of evidence that their use does not necessarily harm the husband-wife relationship (but may even do the couple and their children much good). The debate on private property, the incipient struggle on divorce, homosexuality, masturbation, and suicide likewise show the cumulative impact of new evidence. To use Gustafson's phrase, there are many signs in the Church of an

implicit shift from a "prescriptive" to an "illuminative" use of principles. Contributing to this shift also, of course, has been a reexamination of theological principles and a fresh look at the requirements of the Christian life.[6]

It seems to me that the role of empirical evidence is now forcing a reassessment of the principles that have remained in the ethic of conviction. Moral absolutes, in other words, are having hard days, and are undergoing the same searching reappraisal as the doctrinal absolutes in religion. Yet we should not think that this has not always been so; the evidence might have had to ask for equal time with the absolute, either doctrinal or moral, but eventually it was heard and accommodations were brought about—for example, in examining justified killing, the legitimate taking of someone else's property, in the articulation of the notion of a just war, and how precisely parents are dishonored. Intrinsic values have been altered by a whole series of cases which were gradually permitted to coexist and which came to be no longer considered exceptions to those values.

It would seem, however, that this is a trend which will strengthen in the future development of ethics. In particular, it appears to me that the notion of intrinsic evil or disvalue will meet increasing challenge; it has already been subjected to sterner scrutiny than the concept of intrinsic good. If it can be shown to be untenable, then this in itself is an additional threat to its existence, over and above the evidence that can be adduced against characterizing specific acts as intrinsically wrong. My expectation, therefore, is that a serious re-examination of the notion of intrinsic evil will demonstrate that it is no longer a viable element of contemporary ethical discourse.

[6] Callahan, *loc. cit.*

JOHN COGLEY

11 The Image of Political Man

In the weeks prior to the 1968 presidential nominations, the nation's political commentators and analysts seemed to have been stricken with an acute case of fallibility. So serious was the malady that all most of them saw when they picked up their crystal balls was the shimmering image of a man before a TV camera or typewriter with egg on his face.

They had told us, for example, that Mr. George Romney's campaign in New Hampshire was something to be taken very seriously. Then Mr. Romney abruptly pulled out before the election was held. They had told us that Senator Eugene McCarthy's campaign in New Hampshire was not to be taken seriously, that it was the quixotic, ill-starred effort of a political innocent. There was another surprise, then, when the Minnesota senator's votes were counted. However, we were assured that this was a freak. It could not happen elsewhere. But a few weeks later, word was out that victory for McCarthy was very likely in Wisconsin. More surprise. Then came the famous presidential broadcast on the last day of March, with the stunning news that Mr. Johnson would not accept renomination. Still more surprise. Between these events we had been told to wait for Governor Nelson Rockefeller's routine announcement that he would be a candidate. When the Governor's news conference came, he stated that he would not run.

All in all, the batting average of the big-league seers was not impressive, and most of them were ready to admit it. When Art Buchwald reported on his efforts to get his own crystal ball fixed, he said he found the repair shop crowded with customers, including James Reston, David Lawrence, Robert Novak, Walter Lippmann, Eric Sevareid, William F. Buckley, David Brinkley, Walter Cronkite,

Drew Pearson, Lou Harris, George Gallup, William S. White, and even the clairvoyant Jeanne Dixon.

If all those people could be so wrong, perhaps we should conclude not that they had all lost their analytic talents but that there had been a change in political thinking in the United States and that they were not really plugged into it. Perhaps we are confronted with a new image of political man. I believe so. This new image is just beginning to emerge, but it will probably be dominant for the rest of our lifetime. At least I think that this is the case.

Moreover, I believe that those of us who have been close to religious affairs during the past few years should have seen it coming, and in some cases did. For we knew that the churches have been trying to come to terms with a new image of religious man, and that the politicians sooner or later would be up against the kind of change in political behavior which the religious leaders have had to face in the ecclesiastical world. The churches are aware that laymen no longer think of themselves the way they used to. The clergy and religious, Protestant and Catholic, are going through an identity crisis of their own. I think it would be accurate to say that the bishops and perhaps the Pope himself are also.

These two phenomena, the change in the religious man's self-image and the change in the image of political man, are not unrelated. Many of the same forces have been at work bringing them about. And that, to put it squarely, is my thesis: the "political" image of man that we have lived by so long is being replaced by another image—a theological image of man. At the same time, the traditional theological image of man—the free man, redeemed from every form of spiritual servitude and subjugation to the imperious dictatorship of law and abstractionism—is triumphing over the old image of ecclesiastical man. There are fewer and fewer of that passive creature, subject to the will of others, dependent on them for his religious life, spiritually anemic because he was given the stones of deadening doctrinal formulas and lifeless liturgy when his soul cried out for the bread of a *personal* understanding of divine reality and a genuine sense of liturgical community.

Just as we are already seeing a revolution in the comprehension of religious matters, then, so in the years ahead will we see an unprecedented and profound transformation in political thinking.

That, I realize, is a prediction which I too may someday wish I had never made. Even as I am making it, I keep my fingers crossed. For I have lived long enough in times turbulent enough to know that *all* crystal balls, not merely Reston's or Brinkley's or Pearson's, are clouded, and that this is particularly true when the pace of change has been accelerated to dizzying speed, as it has been in the second half of the twentieth century. I must therefore begin with a disavowal: I have no truly firm confidence that I am capable of discussing politics or the image of political man in the years ahead on any but a speculative basis.

The America of the present is already radically different from the America I grew up in, and vastly different from the country the youngest student in college today has known all his life. Between me and my children, there is a yawning generation gap. But between them and *their* children, there may be a Grand Canyon. The reason is the many-sided revolution moving in on us. The revolution was seeded by our generation and is being carried out by our children's; but our children's children will be attuned to it from birth. It will strike them as neither novel nor revolutionary.

We who have reached our middle years have already begun to feel displaced, at the very time we are supposed to be at the peak of our experience and wisdom. Our children, who have been called on to straddle the dying world of their parents and the evolving world of their own yet-unborn children, are notoriously alienated from the past. Perhaps they will also be alienated from the future. For of all the generations that have grown up in the United States, theirs seems to have been marked to live out their entire lives in a state of collective instability and restlessness.

The reason is simple. They cannot share their parents' pre-World War II perception of human reality on the one hand and on the other the hurricane force of the technological, social, and political changes they will have to face probably means that they have been sentenced to a lifetime of basic uncertainty. Their early upbringing, to be sure, prepared them for rapid changes. But it did not prepare them for the speed or extent of change which it now seems will inevitably confront society in the years ahead.

The children of our children, however, will be different. That they will be notably different from our generation goes without saying, but I suspect they will be almost equally different from the youth of today. For again, the central fact is that politically, psychologically, intellectually, even spiritually, a new man is coming into being—and the present generation of young people has been designated by fate to give this new man birth, to nurture him, civilize him, and hold the world together until he has taken over.

We might hope that today's youth will also truly be able to understand these unborn children of theirs, but there is reason to believe that they may not do much better than we have done in bridging the gap between the generations.

The present revolution—which I will call the post-modern revolution—is worldwide in scope; it is universal in its grasp; and it is profoundly rooted in the human personality. For everything is changing in society, not just political conceptions and economic notions but morals and manners as well. The most important of these changes, I believe, is the transformation in the way people are beginning to think about themselves. Self-images are being radically affected. New modes of thought, new conceptions of human nature, and new beliefs about human destiny have become the mirror in which we see all reality, not excluding political reality. The new way of seeing reality will ultimately revolutionize practically all our institutions, from the family to the university, from the Church to the Communist Party.

It has been said that every revolution devours its own children. When the present revolution comes to fulfillment, I see no reason why the adage will not hold true. Exhaustion is utterly predictable for first-generation revolutionaries. The young who are making the revolution of post-modernity, then, may be its first victims. That, perhaps, is a sad fact of life, but it would be wise to recognize it as well in its totality as also the proud sign of the effectiveness of the first generation's early efforts.

All this, I realize, may sound absurdly apocalyptic. But we are hurling ourselves imaginatively into the future. When I speak of today's youth, the children of our generation, I am not talking about the clear-eyed, tireless, vigorous, openminded, expectant young people they are now. I have another group of men and women in mind, a group still not old—though behind the point after which, as we are now told, trustworthiness can be expected!—but a little less clear-eyed, a little less vigorous, more set in its ways, a great deal more experienced, and notably more burdened with responsibility than they are today.

And if I try to see them twenty years or so older than they are at the present, I must also see them grappling with problems that will face a world yet to be born. Even though perhaps only twenty summers will have passed, that world may also in another sense be eight hundred or a thousand years older than the present world.

The reason, once more, is the fantastic speed of change, the chief characteristic of post-modernity. Progress—at least progress of a scientific and technological kind—is now made in mathematical leaps; the rate of change has become exponential. For the foreseeable future, time will be leapfrogging forward. The world will reach a point of rest, I am confident, but that point lies too far ahead to concern anyone now living.

This, I take it, is what the scientific and technological revolution is all about. This is what the knowledge explosion is all about. This is what the revolution of morals and manners and social arrangements is all about. And it is these revolutions that are shaping a new image of political man.

All these revolutions are actually in their very opening phases. We will have to wait for years before we will see the kind of human being, the new man, they will produce. We have only seen the revolutionary youth; still to come are the youth of the revolution. And these, our children's children, are almost certain to be something else again.

If with this vision of our children's future I cannot project any stability or familiarity—which are barely enjoyed by our generation —I can confidently predict that the challenges they will face will be heroic in dimension. The generational tasks assigned to them will be unprecedented; their success or failure will be crucial for mankind itself.

They are going to be called upon to do new things, things not previously attempted, things not even foreseen for the most part, things that only a few philosophers, a few poets, and a few saints of the past have ever dreamed were even within the power of man. And it is becoming increasingly clear that if these things are not done, mankind's stay on earth may be shorter than we thought it would be.

I would like to accomplish two ends in this discussion. First, I will try to sketch out in broad strokes the tasks that I think lie ahead; and second, I want to delineate the personal characteristics I think will be necessary for political man in the days to come.

Ours is probably the last earthbound generation of man. The most dramatic (but probably not most significant) "new thing" for the next generation will be the leap from the confines of this earth to the distant stars.

I have found a glimmering of what this leap will mean by considering the changes that have taken place in my own lifetime, particularly since World War II and more particularly since the perfection of the jet plane.

Earth distance, it dawned on me recently, is already fairly meaningless. In the past five years alone, I have crossed the Atlantic Ocean about forty times and the United States too many times to keep count. Needless to say, all this has slowly changed my old attitudes.

Within these past fifteen months, for example, I have strolled the broad avenues of Paris; gotten tipsy on red wine with an Olympic star in a Prague tavern; bought the European edition of *The New York Times* from an Italian swinger in St. Peter's Square; walked to Checkpoint Charlie with a Marxist professor in East Berlin; attended a meeting of Spanish Baptist ministers in Madrid; enjoyed old movies in Dublin and new plays in London. And I am speaking only of Europe.

I can just as easily recall particular people, particular buildings, special restaurants, and the distinct smells of certain markets in Cairo, Damascus, Athens, Istanbul, and Jerusalem. Mention Mexico and I think of a particular bar and particular faces. Ask me about Atchison, Kansas and I will warn you against a certain eatery you should avoid. I know a desert spa near Beersheba which accepts Diner's Club cards. I have discovered a place in Los Angeles where *cash* is accepted. Not long ago I realized that the last four haircuts I got were in barbershops separated from one another by no less than a thousand miles.

The point is that the opportunity to travel widely, an opportunity which is becoming more widespread, has made me almost as different from my father, who rarely left home, as my son, who is living at the moment in a village in India, is from me.

I now see the world as a unit. There are no longer any strangers anywhere. I have learned that communications are possible wherever men meet, across lingual, religious, ideological, and cultural borders. I no longer think in such terms as Communist or capitalist, European or African, Arab or Jew. Experience alone has taught me to think rather in terms of the individuals who come under these grand headings. The family of man, I have learned, not from theory alone but from personal confrontations, is precisely that—a family.

If this is true today for a middle-aged, middle-class journalist, think of what it will be like in twenty years. As the reach of man extends, the common humanity of man will become an ever more insistent factor everywhere.

Politics in, say, the 1980s will thus have to be based on a new perception of human reality. The artificial blurrings of the past will
have to be wiped away. The clear image of mankind's oneness,
which theology always upheld but through the ages left vague and
unreal, with few political consequences, will be the starting point
for thought and action concerning human affairs.

A man who would be the political leader of other men in the
years ahead will have to be a leader of mankind itself. Nothing
narrower will do; any less noble or more provincial notion of the
tasks of political leadership will be self-defeating. For technology
has done what all the preachments of the prophets, the prayers of
the saints, the visions of the poets, the principles of the philosophers,
and the teachings of the theologians have not succeeded in doing
through the ages: it has made clear, existentially, palpably clear,
that the secular fate of *all* men is linked together.

Racism, nationalism, religious exclusivism—the spurious divisions
of the world into villains and heroes, superior and inferior kinds of
men, "our own kind" and "foreigners"—are already conspicuously
beside the point, though many of us do not yet realize it. In the years
ahead, the leader who sustains the ancient nationalistic, racial, or
confessional myths on which they were built will be recognized not
merely as an anachronism but as an *enemy* of mankind and a traitor
to those he would lead. It has become brutally evident that the path
of exclusivism is the road to suicide.

We are now witnessing the end of the civil war that has engaged
the energies of the Western world since the French Revolution.
The double fanaticism of political ideology and nationalism, like the
odium theologicum of Protestant-Catholic polemics, is cooling off.
The very existence of nuclear weapons, in the crazy way that history is written straight with crooked lines, was accompanied by the
introduction of at least a measure of rationality into the world of
international politics. The slogan "Make love not war" may still
sound bizarre and flamboyant, but it is basically an appeal to reason,
certainly more rational than, say, the "God wills it" of the Crusades.
Would to God the theologians had said "Make love, not war" con-
vincingly in centuries past—how much bloodshed and misery and
terror mankind would have been spared! If the slogan can be translated into meaningful political terms, its essential rationality will be
evident to all.

However, we recognize that the tribal myths of exclusivism still
hang on, stubbornly resisting the death already overdue for them;

their continuing existence is the major reason none of us is ever sure that rationality will not momentarily fail and that the day's sun may not set on a world half devastated by the force of nuclear energy.

Since August, 1945, we have lived with this kind of uncertainty. We have survived, though on occasion merely by the skin of our teeth. But when space travel with its implications becomes comparatively commonplace, we can no longer depend on this catch-as-catch-can survival. Unless mankind lifts it thoughts beyond the petty parochialism and sectarian spirit that up to now has led again and again to human carnage, there will be no men for political leaders to lead.

I would argue, then, that politics in the future will have to be totally oblivious of racial differences, nationalistic prejudices, and cultural biases. Men able to look upon the earth from the stellar context, as the next generation certainly will, will need a god's-eye view of humanity. They cannot in any basic sense be a leader of black, white, or yellow men; their words and deeds will have to indicate concern for all men, everywhere.

We are already moving in that direction. There are signs of it in the agonizing death of racism. Every poll shows that the young are significantly less racially prejudiced than their parents. Despite brutal setbacks, the unity of all men is being more securely forged.

On college campuses all over the United States, for example, students in recent years summoned their courage and moral indignation to protest against the bombing and killing of unknown yellow men in far-off Vietnam, and were outraged by the sterile syllogisms of political leaders and prelates alike. That would not have happened even ten years ago. It is evident that the tribal slogans of old are losing their power.

Appeals to support a crusade against communism, where the young are concerned, fall more and more on deaf ears. Patriotic and nationalistic slogans, with their exclusivist appeal, have lost their punch—to the consternation of many men of my generation who were brought up on them. Ideological and theological war chants, whether issuing from the White House, the Kremlin, or the Chancery Office, now sound hollow and unconvincing in the light of the consciousness of mankind's oneness sweeping across the globe.

This, at least in part, is how I read the feeling of togetherness, the sense of generation, that now unites youth everywhere. The young in all corners of the globe are joining hands as human beings rather than as Negroes or whites, Christians or atheists, Communists or capitalists, Occidentals or Orientals. More and more people in the rising generation have declared war on war. More and more are figuratively burning their old racial, confessional, ideological, and nationalistic draft cards and have decided to join the human race.

The movement may still be only a stream running through political thought. I would hazard the prediction, however, that soon it will be a mighty torrent of sentiment and conviction throughout the world.

The leaders of the future, then, will have to take this new view of humanity into account. Belief on the part of many that the sense of common humanity transcends the ancient slogans of war and threats of war certainly made life difficult for President Johnson and his associates. It is also making life difficult for the leaders of the Communist empire, as I have learned in travels throughout that part of the world. And its reach is not only horizontal but vertical. It provides reason for strain and division between old and young, in the home, on college and university campuses, in churches, and not least of all in the councils of political parties.

President John F. Kennedy, I believe, had a glimpse of this new realization of mankind as a unity, though he too was hampered by older commitments and outmoded ways of doing things. Nevertheless, there were indications that he was beginning to look upon the role of leadership as a universal rather than a tribal assignment. His grasp of the new demands of leadership did not go unnoticed or unappreciated—especially by the young. Throughout the world, in friendly and "enemy" countries alike, his memory is revered over all others for this reason.

Unfortunately, Mr. Kennedy's successor gave the impression of being unalterably stuck in the thought grooves of an earlier day. He paid the price. Before his announcement that he would not run again, Mr. Johnson proved to be a leader with a diminishing number of followers in his own country and few elsewhere, especially among the young. It became clear that in what he wanted to be a steady journey toward an honored place in history he was held up, not only at Credibility Gap but at Generation Gap as well.

And that, I believe, is one of the most telling reasons President Johnson's leadership lagged so far behind our earlier expectations. He was not able to see the requirements of leadership in an age when, in his predecessor's words, we have to put an end to war— which implies an end to a narrow, provincial, nationalistic conception of political reality—or war will put an end to us. But that knowledge is very much with those who will be in the position of leadership in the decades to come.

The next generation, I am convinced, has a firm hold on this insight. Put into effect, shaping minds, attitudes, and expectations, it will revolutionize society. The man who is not prepared in the future for a *mondialized* mankind will simply not be a leader; for he will be talking a language—whether it is accented with old-fashioned racism, drip-dry patriotism, syllogistic theology, or frozen-crystal ideology—that the world, thanks be to God, will no longer understand, or at least will refuse to listen to seriously.

I have emphasized mankind's growing realization that it is, together, only one family. Another sign of the times is equally basic, equally important. I have in mind the growing awareness of individuals everywhere of what it means to be human, simply human. More and more, young people are deciding to take their personal destinies into their own hands—to break with convention when convention strikes them as meaningless; to question moral standards when they find no reasonable basis for upholding them; to figure out for themselves what is worthy of their spiritual loyalty; to resist the Establishment, whether political, social, corporate, military, educational, or ecclesiastic, when it strikes them as self-perpetuating or self-seeking; to question values long taken for granted, setting out on their own in the pursuit of meaningfulness. In a word, young people today are intent above all on being themselves, and there is every reason to believe the tendency will soon be fully dominant.

In this new way of reckoning, the goal of life is looked upon as building a self worthy of respect. Though undeniably it has led to some absurd posturing, self-deception, mindless rebellion, and a library of thoughtless slogans that pass for avant-garde thought, the trend is basically good. We have to remember that every lasting movement began with an excess of zeal—for example, the emancipation of women, Marxism, even Christianity. There is no reason that we should expect the movement for self-realization to be entirely free of grotesque expression. Nevertheless, the movement is here to stay. More and more it will determine the nature of political leadership. Within the next twenty years or so, it will be a decisive factor. No politician, educator, cultural leader, or churchman will be able to ignore it.

There are signs everywhere that many of the traditional canons of leadership have already been outmoded. The man who would lead others is already finding out that, at least where the younger generation is concerned, he can get nowhere until he understands the growth in human awareness of what it actually means to be a human being. His own task, he already knows, though he does not know quite what to do about it, is not to lay down the law; it is to show others how their desire to be themselves can be creatively implemented for the good of all rather than employed destructively against society itself. In the years to come, that task will almost be a definition of a leader—one who is able to show people how to work *with* others and *for* others without sacrificing their own individuality, betraying their private values, or silencing their sense of wrong and right.

The revolutionary *personalist* tendency in the world will inevitably be expanded, now that it is underway. Basic notions of the political order are being challenged by it. With the coming of the affluent society, the fundamental purpose of political action is being seen in a new light. Politics, which was long regarded as fundamentally a way of insuring economic well-being, is increasingly considered as the way to insure the good life in all senses for all. In political thinking there has been a radical change in emphasis from fighting physical poverty exclusively to combating psychological poverty. Ancient theological questions are being asked anew in the name of politics—questions about happiness, morality, and the responsibility one has for others—on every university campus in the nation and to some degree already in the halls of Congress, the executive suites of Madison Avenue, and the board rooms of Wall Street.

For example: How to make law an instrument for the liberation of the individual as he understands himself, not as he was abstractly defined in an age that has passed? How to control technology in an America that has been transformed from an industrial society to one directed by technology and information theory, so that technology serves human needs while neither dehumanizing us nor threatening to destroy us? How to organize the world politically so that the different branches of the human family do not menace but enrich one another? How to restructure education for a technological age when almost all the tasks that take up our time even today will be handled by machines, and the average man's leisure will be incredibly expanded? How to lift the corrupting boredom already burdening technologized man and threatening to overwhelm him completely?

How to redistribute the world's good so that the masses soon to be born in underdeveloped countries can be furnished food and shelter, not even to mention the amenities of education and culture that are their due as men? (According to present projections, the gross national product of the United States in 1985 will be $1.4 trillion—three times that of the Soviet Union and hundreds of times that of the poorer nations, which will be getting poorer as we get richer.) How to control population growth? How to bring the advantages of literacy, technology, and scientific progress where they are most needed, and how to reconstruct the medical profession to make it possible for most of mankind to enjoy the benefits of modern science?

These are only some of the questions that loom over the rising generation. And judging by contemporary events, the young people will demand a voice in the solutions. More and more young men and women are no longer content to let remote leaders control their destinies from behind closed doors. The present student population is providing a sample of what to expect in the coming years when most of our citizens will insist on having a personal say about every public decision affecting their private lives or representing their thinking.

Up to now, this determination to be heard has led to conflicts between civil authorities and dissenting citizens—to rioting, violence, even civil chaos. Rioting and violence are certainly to be deplored, if only because they dehumanize those participating in them. But denunciation will not in itself, as we are painfully learning, resolve the problem of how to maintain order, protect life and property, and yet uphold the freedom to participate in democratic decision-making.

Given that the political participation movement is here to stay and that it represents the next great development in political behavior, as I believe, the need for creative leadership has never been more critical than it will be in the years immediately ahead. New methods of decision-making will have to be devised, new safeguards for the protection of both the individual person and the body politic will have to be established, new concepts of political leadership will have to be invented.

The response of political leaders to these developments has in the main been sheer bafflement and blind reaction. The reason is that there has been so little understanding of what is actually happening, not primarily in the political arena but in man's internal life: the astounding growth in self-awareness I am talking about is the heart of the matter, and this new element has changed the entire political and social algebraic. Until leadership catches up with the inward change, social imbalance is only to be expected.

It seems terribly clear that within a decade our social and political institutions will be hopeless if they are not radically revamped to suit the radical change in human awareness already under way. And in this monumental transformation, religious thinking has a role to play—if it will assume the responsibility. For there is no doubt that the political and theological tasks have been intertwined. It is not altogether flattering to the theologians that so many people have had to learn the central humane lessons of theology via political action. We know that while the religiously alienated have said, "Make love, not war," many, too many religious spokesmen have been spokesmen for militarism. We know that political action, often led by agnostics and atheists, did more for interracial justice in a few years than was accomplished by the tonguetied churches during a hundred years of silent collaboration with segregation. We know how much the political enterprise taught a reluctant Church about freedom of religion and is still teaching it about democratic procedures and personal liberty.

From the point of view of institutional religion, it is a matter of shame and scandal that political leaders have so often been so far ahead in communicating ideals that are basically theological. I know that I have learned more about the social meaning of my faith from political spokesmen than from bishops, pastors, or theologians.

But this need not go on forever. I still think theology has something to offer the political enterprise. But to give it, theology must revolutionize itself—to lead rather than follow, to use its treasures rather than hoard them, to liberate itself from its own prison of conformity, fear, and the dead abstractionism of the past.

JACK VAUGHN

12 Tilting at Treadmills

With the aim of provoking thought (though at the risk of provoking stupefaction), I should like to quote a sentence of congressional prose—a 110-word sentence with only four commas in it.

It is section 2 of Title I of the Peace Corps Act of 1961. Its heading is "Declaration of Purpose," and it goes like this:

> The Congress of the United States declares that it is the policy of the United States and the purpose of this Act to promote world peace and friendship through a Peace Corps, which shall make available to interested countries and areas men and women of the United States qualified for service abroad and willing to serve, under conditions of hardship if necessary, to help the people of such countries and areas in meeting their needs for trained manpower, and to help promote a better understanding of the American people on the part of the peoples served and a better understanding of other peoples on the part of the American people.

I cite this sentence not for its elegant syntax, its rich imagery, or its lyrical flow of language—in case you were wondering. I cite it because, for all its bulk, it is a serviceable carryall for the ideas that have animated the Peace Corps since its founding.[1]

I propose now to unpack some of those ideas so that they can be looked at closely. It seems to me that this is a good way of describing what we are doing or trying to do.

More important, I think that a close look at those ideas will substantiate our conviction that, even during a time when Americans are fighting abroad and facing civil disorder at home—in fact, especially during such a time—what the Peace Corps is trying to do is very much to the point.

[1] March 1, 1961, by executive order of President John F. Kennedy.

The first idea is that "peace" and "friendship" are inextricably intertwined, if indeed they are not simply two ways of saying the same thing.

I don't suppose that this comes as stop-press news. But then, it is not its novelty that makes this idea a crucial and a challenging one today in every part of the world. On the contrary, what is remarkable—and tragic—is that ancient as this idea is, elementary as it is, incontrovertible as it is, it is so often and so flagrantly ignored.

No rational man thinks that the way to make friends is to lock his doors, bar his windows, arm himself to the teeth, and post threatening notices on his fence; or to meddle, uninvited, in his neighbors' affairs; or to boast of the purity of his motives, the superiority of his culture, and the stubbornness of his will.

Yet throughout the world, presumably rational men justify precisely such actions with the argument that they lead to peace.

They do not, of course.

Even if such expedients as "cold war" or "brinkmanship" or "the balance of terror"—the phrases get more nerve-racking year by year, doubtless because year by year our anxiety over how dangerously we live increases—do keep us from destroying ourselves in one fell swoop, they are not peace or anything like peace. The most they do is buy time during which to strive for peace. And we scarcely need reminding that the amount of time they can buy is limited, that hostile feelings, if they persist, will sooner or later express themselves, and that weapons, if they are not laid aside, will sooner or later be used.

Peace is a condition in which men and women rely upon and trust one another; in which they deal openly and unfearfully with one another; in which they share one another's interests and concerns; in which they respect one another's customs and points of view; in which they are friends. At bottom, achieving peace means changing—indeed, uplifting—the minds and habits of men.

Sometimes I am asked why our organization is called the *Peace* Corps, although volunteers are not potentates or diplomats. They are teachers and farmers and workers in public health and community development who negotiate no treaties, deliver no notes, compose no white papers, compile no dossiers, and have no power to start wars or stop them.

Well, the beginning of the answer to that question is that we are the Peace Corps because the objective of everything we do is to make worldwide friendship possible.

By this I do not merely mean that, whatever a volunteer's specific duties are, he can perform them only if he is accepted as a friend by people to whom he was at first a stranger—and I might comment in passing that in dozens of the world's languages, the word for "stranger" is the same as the word for "enemy." Certainly, volunteers are (or should be) friendly; for that matter, they also are (or should be) trustworthy, loyal, helpful, courteous, kind, cheerful, obedient, thrifty, brave, clean, and reverent.

And if I sound facetious, it is not because I doubt that man-to-man friendships are important to peace. On the contrary, I believe firmly that every time two strangers from widely different cultures become friends, they add a mite to peace; and I am inclined to believe also that enduring peace has to be built mite by mite.

The difficulty, of course, is that in a world in which there are fourteen thousand Peace Corps volunteers and several million men actively pursuing the profession of arms, it would be foolish to pretend that the personal friends we make are numerous enough, by themselves, to affect the immediate course of events. This is particularly so since our friends are Micronesian fishermen and Bolivian shepherds and Malaysian rice farmers and African school children, people who have no more present power than Peace Corps volunteers to start or stop wars.

Our conception of worldwide friendship extends far beyond the personal friendships we are able to make, rewarding and worthwhile as those are.

Which brings me to a second important idea in that long congressional sentence: that helping underdeveloped nations is the real way to peace.

The least important implication of this idea is that sending upright and generous young Americans to serve overseas helps destroy that "ugly American" image over which so many hands have been wrung in recent years. Wounding as it may be to the vanity of Americans to be thought of as ugly—or for that matter, irksome as it may be to American diplomats and businessmen and tourists overseas as they make their daily rounds—no one who inquires seriously into the causes of the tension and hostility and violence that exist in the world can think that "the ugly American" is an important one.

And in any case, if "ugly American" is more than an expedient catch phrase that critics of America's foreign policy use to personify that policy, if most Americans overseas (except upright and generous Peace Corps volunteers, of course) really are ugly, they should be brought home and replaced with beautiful Americans, not merely offset with Peace Corps volunteers.

No, the Peace Corps is not in the image-building or image-destroying business. It is attempting to deal with reality, not images. I said a few paragraphs above that achieving peace means changing the minds and habits of men. It also means changing the conditions in which men live, for the way their minds work and the way they habitually behave are closely bound up with whether they are rich or poor, educated or ignorant, free or oppressed. Without world-wide prosperity and knowledge and freedom, there can be no lasting worldwide peace.

What does this mean in practical terms?

It means that gross inequalities between nations are not only deplorable but dangerous.

It means that when a few nations are very rich and well-organized and strong and most of the rest are very poor and disorganized and weak, some of the weak nations are bound to become envious or foolhardy or servile and some of the strong ones are bound to become manipulative or arrogant or rapacious.

It means that an underdeveloped country is always up for grabs —whether from the outside by a power-hungry large nation or a greedy small one, or from the inside by a power-hungry and greedy tyrant.

It means even that the sheer physical survival of the human race may ultimately hinge on whether or not the underdeveloped countries are able to develop themselves—and I stress "themselves." Development must be a do-it-yourself project, because dignity and self-reliance are also essential to peace.

The Peace Corps is dedicated to helping underdeveloped countries search for ways to develop themselves. That is the heart of the connection between the Peace Corps and peace.

And, I must add, I am more than a little impatient with those who see something hypocritical in the fact that fourteen thousand American volunteers are working for peace in fifty-seven underdeveloped countries, some of them huge, at the same time as half a million American troops are fighting in one small underdeveloped country, Vietnam.

The war in Vietnam is an awful illustration of what can happen when a country is up for grabs—and both the supporters and the critics of our Vietnam policy should be able to agree to that, even though they disagree vehemently about the identity of the principal grabber.

The war in Vietnam does not mock the Peace Corps's mission. Quite to the contrary, it makes it more real, more relevant, more urgent than it ever has been. For what our volunteers are doing is participating in the effort of fifty-seven countries to become—often against long odds—masters of their fate rather than victims of it, like Vietnam.

The next thing I shall pull out of the congressional carryall is its characterization of the countries where the Peace Corps goes: "interested" countries. It may be a weak word, but a strong idea is behind it: there is all the difference in the world between voluntary service and gratuitous service. Volunteers go only where they are needed and wanted and invited.

Adherence to this principle is what distinguishes Peace Corps work from do-goodism, the insistence on helping people whether or not they want to be helped, the insistence that the helper knows more than the helped about what kind of help to give.

There are no "Peace Corps programs" overseas. There are Bolivian programs and Philippine programs and Ethiopian programs, and so on to the number of fifty-seven, in which volunteers are invited to take part. We don't decide what the programs are, and we don't run them. If we can, we do what our hosts ask us to do. If we can't, we confess our incapacity and stay away.

This does not mean, of course, that we do not try to play a constructive part in designing programs that involve volunteers. One of the little-told tales of the Peace Corps is how creatively our overseas staff people contribute to the development efforts of fifty-seven countries. But they make this contribution as partners with their hosts in furthering their hosts' interests, not as representatives of America's or Americans' interests.

I am dwelling on this point because, simple as it seems to all of us in the Peace Corps, it is terribly hard to persuade certain people that we are not practicing what they call "cultural imperialism," that we are not trying in some naive or sneaky way to impose American social and economic and political standards on the under-

developed world. Sometimes it seems to me that those who make
this charge are operating on the assumption that every American
standard is—or should be—anathema to the underdeveloped world.

Now, it is true, of course, that there are aspects of American life
which *are* anathema in a few or in many countries. Much of our
foreign policy is widely deplored. Our treatment of our black
citizens over the centuries is almost universally scorned and con-
demned. Our mechanized mass culture is often ridiculed. Our preoccupation with worldly goods is sometimes regarded with con-
tempt. Well, I need not go on. I'm sure everyone reading these
words has at the tip of his tongue a long personal list of American
failings—and I know every Peace Corps volunteer does, too.

However, there are other things about America that the progressive leaders of the underdeveloped world and many of the men in
the street as well do not merely admire but are desperately interested
in emulating: the stability of our political institutions, the produc-
tivity of our economy, the universality of our education, the social
mobility of most of our population.

In some ways, America is a model for the underdeveloped world,
and a pretty revolutionary model at that, in the context of their
customs and institutions. It is not revolutionary because it is in-
dustrialized and mechanized and urbanized and computerized and
sanitized and homogenized. Peace Corps volunteers are not invited
overseas to bring the underdeveloped world those blessings, although
there are plenty of countries that would like to have more industry
and more organization and, for that matter, more sanitation. Plumb-
ing may be funny, but it isn't an unmitigated evil.

But a chief reason Peace Corps volunteers *are* invited overseas is
the hope by the leaders of fifty-seven countries that certain American attitudes—purposefulness, daring, self-confidence, optimism—
will be contagious. They have been invited, in other words, not in
spite of being Americans but because they are Americans. If we are
bringing American culture overseas, it is because our hosts not only
want us to but urge us to.

It has often been suggested that the Peace Corps be international-
ized. There are major political, administrative, and logistical obstacles
to such a move, but I can imagine no objection to it in principle—
providing that within an international framework, the distinctive
national qualities of volunteers from each nation could be cherished
and used.

And so we come to the most interesting part of the Peace Corps story: the specific nature of the contribution that a handful of volunteers, most of them just out of college and many of them without real technical skills, can and do make to development.

A clue comes toward the end of my congressional sentence—the part that talks about "the American people" (not "America" or "the American government") and "other peoples" (not "other nations" or "other governments").

What is distinctive about the Peace Corps is that its direct—indeed, its entire—concern is with people, with individual men, women, and children. A volunteer's work is personal in every way. His tools are his personal qualities: his courage and patience and optimism and insight. His working technique is to establish personal relationships with those around him. And, most important by far, his purpose is to help individual human beings find ways to lead full and meaningful lives.

This last point is one that I want to explore for a moment, for it isn't dwelt upon nearly enough in discussions of underdevelopment. Underdevelopment is commonly described in terms of gross national product and mean annual income and infant mortality rate and average yield per acre and number of road miles and incidence of illiteracy and so on and on—a veritable symphony of statistics.

The trouble is that development programs based solely on a strictly economic statistical or quantitative approach just don't work, and everybody knows this by now: the Congress, which every year reduces foreign aid authorizations and appropriations; the American people, who every year take a more sour and pessimistic view of what foreign aid has accomplished or can accomplish; the governments and the peoples of other rich and developed countries, which every year show less interest in participating in development efforts; and the thoughtful leaders of the underdeveloped countries themselves, who every year put more stress on changing attitudes and institutions than on building factories and airports, on gently adapting their cultures to the twentieth century than on forcing their cultures into Western molds, on devising distinctive and indigenous responses to their needs than on copying the way rich nations conduct themselves.

Let me quote a short passage from the prologue of Gunnar Myrdal's brilliant new study of South Asia, *Asian Drama*:

. . . while in the Western world an analysis in "economic" terms —markets and prices, employment and unemployment, consumption and savings, investment and output—that abstracts from attitudes, institutions and culture may make sense and lead to valid inferences, an analogous procedure plainly does not in underdeveloped countries. There one cannot make such abstractions; a realistic analysis must deal with the problems in terms that are attitudinal and institutional and take into account the very low levels of living and culture.[2]

It is a passage crammed with complicated thoughts, and I shall concentrate on only one of them: that a realistic account or analysis of underdevelopment must include a description of the lives that men, women, and children live.

Most of them lead existences of deprivation, of unfulfillment, of futility.

There may be a "happy native" here or there, but he is not easy to find. The people who are easy to find are the millions who want a better life and who need help to get it—which is another reason that the notion of "cultural imperialism" is absurd.

Now, I don't want to generalize too broadly about the actual physical circumstances of life in fifty-seven countries because, obviously, in no one of them is the situation precisely like that in any other.

Some countries where volunteers work are able to feed themselves and some are not. Some are ravaged by disease and some are relatively unplagued. Some have quite extensive school and university systems and some provide almost no education. Some have a considerable middle class and some merely a tiny elite and a huge peasant population. Some have nationwide political and social institutions that function more or less coherently and some are a mosaic of separate, often violently hostile families, tribes, and sects. Some are democracies and some are dictatorships, and some of the dictatorships are fairer and more humane than some of the nominal democracies. Some can truthfully be called developing or emerging and some show almost no signs of growth.

And so material and cultural deprivation in the underdeveloped world extends over a very broad spectrum. It can be almost absolute: not enough food, no medical care, no schools. Or it can be relative: a less than fair share of the goods and services that are on hand, and inadequate opportunity or skill or power to redress the balance.

And may I add, not at all parenthetically, that we Americans

[2] Gunnar Myrdal, *Asian Drama: An Inquiry into the Poverty of Nations*, 3 vols., New York, Twentieth Century Fund, 1968, vol. I.

have reason to know that the second kind of deprivation, though not so heartrending, is far more explosive than the first.

All varieties of deprivation breed attitudes or states of mind that in turn reinforce the deprivation, so that living becomes an endless trudge on a treadmill: no matter how hard you pump your legs, you don't advance an inch.

Let me try to illustrate. In virtually every part of the underdeveloped world—in the mountains of South America, on the plains of India, in the Malaysian jungle and the African bush—there are multitudes of farmers who use methods of cultivation that are primitive and backbreaking and grossly unproductive.

Such farmers contribute less than they might, if they contribute at all, to feeding the nonfarm population or to increasing their countries' exports; and of course, they earn little or no cash income for themselves. They live in poverty. They also live of necessity in superstitious anxiety or in stolid, fatalistic, impregnable resignation, for a single flood, drought, epidemic, or insect plague can quite literally wipe them off the face of the earth.

The fear and fatalism have as much to do with the kind of farming they do as their lack of fertilizers and pesticides and improved seeds and modern implements and technical expertise. That has been proved at a cost of hundreds of millions of dollars over the last couple of decades. Time after time in place after place, the United States Agency for International Development, the United Nations Food and Agricultural Organization, or a local ministry of agriculture has presented to such farmers the materials and the advice they so badly need. Far more often than not, nothing has come of it: plows have rusted in the fields, seeds have rotted in the sheds, instructions have been forgotten as soon as the instructor left town. The farmers simply did not have enough courage or self-reliance or faith or hope to use them. They did not dare to change their ways. They suffered a veritable paralysis of will.

In sum, poverty and ignorance breed fear and fatalism, and fear and fatalism freeze people into poverty and ignorance.

That's one kind of treadmill.

Sometimes there is an escape from it, if there happens to be a school around, and a child is bright, and his parents are ambitious for him and can manage without his labor.

Education: that sounds like just the ticket, doesn't it, for elevating both the aspirations and the capabilities of people like the deprived farmers I have been speaking of? Unfortunately, much more often than not, it isn't, and for reasons that go far beyond the acute short-age of schools and teachers so many nations suffer under.

Sometimes education in the underdeveloped world is wildly in-appropriate in both what and how it teaches. This is particularly true in countries that were colonies until a few years ago and where schools have not yet had an opportunity to change much. For the object of colonial education was quite the reverse of producing thinkers or analysts or problem-solvers or, for that matter, strong and independent men. Its object was to produce a docile class of petty civil servants who could file correspondence, stamp docu-ments, and act as buffers between the authorities and the "natives."

Under this system, there was a watershed in every schoolchild's life: the final examination. If he crossed it successfully, he was a white-collar worker for life; if he didn't, his chances for improving his lot were all but completely gone. The reason he studied was to pass the examination. His whole school experience discouraged him from having any motive more elevated than that.

Consequently, many African schoolboys, to give one example, still are learning by rote the succession of the kings of England and the provisions of the Magna Charta—which don't help them much if they go back to the farm.

But of course, the chief point is that school graduates in the underdeveloped world seldom do go back to the farm, even if they have graduated from an agricultural school. Far more damaging than whatever absurdities of curriculum and pedagogy there may be is a common attitude toward education: that it is training not for ad-dressing hard contemporary problems but for avoiding them, that it is a means not of lifting a nation out of squalor and frustration but of personal escape from squalor and frustration.

There are progressive officials in every country who work tire-lessly to change this attitude, but all too many schoolchildren, par-ents, and even classroom teachers look upon a diploma as an official exemption from physical labor, from living in a village, from any difficult or disagreeable line of work or way of life.

In other words, education can do the reverse of providing trained and enlightened men and women for an underdeveloped country; it can remove the brightest and most talented people from just those activities and those places where they are most urgently needed. And of course, an education system that does this is very hard to change because it is the chief supplier of its own manpower—teachers and officials.

That's another kind of treadmill.

I'll describe one other kind, then I'll get off the treadmill.

In a number of the underdeveloped countries, women, by long and hallowed tradition, are in a state of almost complete subjugation. They are given no education, no voice in communal affairs, no personal rights. They spend their days in household drudgery. They may leave their houses only if they wear garments that envelop them from head to toe and make them almost immobile. Their husbands have life-and-death powers over them.

Now, clearly, treating women this way not only constitutes an unpardonable affront to their dignity, not to say their humanity, but seriously retards the process of development. The great amount of work needed in an underdeveloped country cannot be done if half the population is forbidden to take part in it. The free institutions that must be built cannot be when half the population is in bondage. And above all, children will not grow up to become the bold, enlightened young men and women that every underdeveloped country needs more than it needs anything else if they are raised by dull and timid drudges.

It is conditions and attitudes like those I have described that Peace Corps volunteers meet and attempt to cope with—and no other group of Americans overseas does.

You might say they tilt at treadmills.

They do it any way they can. They do it by precept and by example; by persuading timid people to dare, and tradition-bound people to change their ways; by showing that educated men and women can live in huts and work with their hands without losing their dignity; by teaching children to think rather than recite; by proving that women who show their faces (and legs) and do useful work need not be ashamed—or shameless; by involving themselves every day in the everyday cares and pleasures of thousands of communities.

It is person-to-person work. It has to be. Proclamations and statutes and economic analyses and technical syllabuses and five-year plans have little effect on attitudes and customs. Full-time workers on the scene have a big one.

Who can say with statistics what Peace Corps volunteers have done? I cannot claim that their efforts show in the gross national product, the mean annual income, the infant mortality rate, the average yield per acre, the number of road miles, or the incidence of illiteracy in any country, even the smallest one.

And I do not believe that the really important things volunteers do ever will show in such statistics, even if someday volunteers blanket the earth.

The lives of tens of thousands of men, women, and children in every part of the world are more purposeful and fulfilled today than they were before the Peace Corps touched them. But who can quantify purpose and fulfillment?

The minds of tens of thousands of men, women, and children in every part of the world are more open today than they were before the Peace Corps touched them. But who can chart the opening of a mind?

Perhaps at some time during the last eight years in some village classroom, a volunteer has helped rouse the sleeping mind and spirit of a child who is destined to become, a generation from now, another Simón Bolívar or Mohandas Gandhi or Julius Nyerere. If he did, if just one volunteer did just that one thing—and the possibility is not all that far-fetched—the Peace Corps will have contributed more to the underdeveloped world than all the AID and FAO and WHO and other alphabetical and nonalphabetical development programs combined.

But no one will ever know. No one will ever know for sure precisely what any volunteer has done, least of all the volunteer himself. If and when the seeds he has planted sprout, he will be long gone.

What I do know for sure is that in a world filled with childish prattle and childish belligerence and childish egotism and childish greed, Peace Corps volunteers conduct themselves with the dignity and assume the responsibilities and do the work of men.

V Closing Observation

REV. CHARLES KOHLI

13 A Time To Be at One

Romano Guardini spoke in *The Lord* of the conversion of the spoken word into the written. He said that the process is fatal to the tone and intention of the original. His own book proves him wrong, but that may not be so for this chapter. It represents the substance of a sermon preached at a Eucharist at which the editor of this volume was present.

The text of the sermon and the difficulty of preaching it were due to a special set of circumstances. The Eucharist was held in the chapel of a private school; the congregation was formed of the teachers, religious and lay, and a few invited guests. The occasion was the conclusion of a day of study and prayer that was to initiate and consecrate the work of the incipient school year. With an enthusiasm—a fervor, I might say—which I found deeply admirable, the committee in charge had composed a liturgy that was to express the event and the faith of the celebrating community. When this was made known to me, I had the difficult task of telling the community that I could not in conscience use its liturgy.

It became obvious that preaching at this Eucharist would be a highly "relevant action," an interpretation and in a sense a justification of a sacramental act, which some would consider self-consciously legalistic and others might consider a rebuff to their own conscientious attempt to be obedient to the Spirit.

When I decided that I could not use the liturgy presented, I decided to use the Votive Mass for Christian Unity. The homily became not simply an attempt to unfold the texts but a plea for an understanding of the "rubrical" approach to the Eucharist as a manifestation of the fact that the Church, the *visible* Church, is the valid context of eucharistic celebration. My motivation in this sermon was strongly influenced by my present evaluation of past convictions of a very different nature. I was not concerned for legal demands for their own sake, but rather desirous of communicating my own discovery that the life celebrated in the Eucharist is the life of the Church itself and that unity with the visible hierarchical Church seemed the best guarantee of having life to celebrate. This seemed particularly important since the time was that of the initial explosion over the encyclical *Humanae vitae*. The signs of disunity and possible schism were all around. It seemed important to emphasize by every possible means that the Thomistic and biblical conception of the reality of the Eucharist, *res sacramenti*, centered on unity with "those who hold and teach the Catholic faith that comes to us from the apostles." I felt that it was this which preaching should communicate and sacrament should celebrate.

All of this seemed even more immediately pertinent because of the identity of the congregation. I wanted to emphasize to a group of teachers that their prophetic function could have no more effective expression than their witness to and creation of the unity of the Body of Christ springing from His mind, which Catholic Christians see as also "the mind of the Church."

What follows, therefore, is substantially the text of the sermon. No attempt has been made to change its homiletic form into that of a theological tract.

The text of the mass which you submitted for this celebration is a very beautiful one. It is deeply expressive of concern for life and growth in the Church; it is filled with real openness to the Word and to the Spirit Who brings that Word to the level of understanding in us. In my own conscience, however—and I speak as the one who must preside at this assembly—it has one unsurmountable flaw. It does not belong to the Church. It is, I would suggest, an expression of the climate which we have come to call that of the "underground." I would like to explain to you why I did not feel that we could use it; I would like even more to be able to communicate to you why I feel that the grace of this time is that we should rejoice to be at one with the Church in its life and worship. I feel that the day has come when this joy should drive concerned Christians out of any caverns underground into what I believe to be the strong and surprising sunlight of the Church's new day.

I do not wish now to emphasize liturgical forms. I would like, however, to be a bit of a phenomenologist. I would like to speak of the external realities as symptoms of the life which they express.

We are all aware that there are varieties of eucharistic expression used in our metropolitan area. University churches are using their own liturgies; groups of Christians in home Eucharists are "hanging loose from the structure" in their worship forms. Please believe me when I say that this sermon is not *about them*. I have neither the charism nor the office to be a judge of anyone; I am a preacher, not a bishop. This sermon is about us, about you and me. It is an invitation to examine our role at this Eucharist, here and now. As Christian and as priest, I have both a conscience and a chance to speak. I ask to share with you my own reasons for not using your liturgy and to invite you to share my own conviction that there is no deeper grace in this Eucharist than that of celebrating our life in the unity of the Church. I know of no better way of doing so than to use the Church's own form for this celebration.

Many of us who were young priests before the Second Vatican Council had our own fling with the heady excitement of experimentation with the liturgy. I was no stranger to these experiences, but I have come to a very different conviction from that of past years. It is one which I see not as a hangup but as a discovery of great freedom and great certainty. I want to share with you my conviction that in celebrating the Eucharist in the way prescribed for us by the Council, the rubrics, and the Bishop, we are set free from many limitations of our own into the dynamic life of the universal Church, the vine and Body of the Lord Jesus. The great thanksgiving is our celebration of the gift and vocation of membership in Him. The structure of the Church is the structure of His Body; belonging to that structure and celebrating its sacrament are at the center of the joy of the Catholic Christian. As I understand it, what we celebrate at the Eucharist is unity with Jesus precisely in the unity of His Church. That Church is the structure, the institution, the Body in which He speaks to us through the Pope and the bishops in communion with him—men themselves in historical communion with those through whom the faith of the Church has been handed down from the beginning.

Saint Paul and Saint Thomas, preachers and theologians from two periods of the *paradosis*, the process of tradition that began with the Scriptures, remind us that the point, the *res* of the Eucharist is the mystery of the Church. Paul states that the oneness of the Bread is the sign and source of the unity of the Body. Consequently, he is saying also that the unity of the Body is the context for the celebration of the Lord's table. Thomas says precisely the same thing when he holds that the *res sacramenti* is the unity of the Church, the whole Christ. It is this that makes it unthinkable to me for us to go underground, to hide from the Church as we celebrate the Eucharist. It is the Church itself that we celebrate here, our gathering together as those given in this life the grace of knowing the peace of the new creation. It is in the Church that I find this peace; it is in and with the Church that I celebrate this peace; to the extent to which I cut myself off from the Church, I fear that I will lose this peace.

We have all spoken much in the last few years of the fallacy of the "Jesus and I" approach to Christian life. I think that we now need to study the dimensions of the "Jesus and we" which is the correct perspective. This involves a careful and consistent theology of the Church. It also demands a similarly precise theology of the Eucharist.

What we celebrate at this table is not only the presence and the accepted sacrifice of the living and risen Jesus. We celebrate as well the reality and the sacrifice of the Church which is His Body. The Church of the New Testament, the Church of history since Pentecost, the Church of *now*—it is this Church whose life we celebrate as we stand here gathered at the Lord's table. It is this historical Church that is anointed and sent to be light for the world and salt for the earth. It is this Church that is the prophetic Body of the Word by baptism and confirmation. It is this Church that gives us both the right and the reason to make a Eucharist. Our anointing, our mission, our vocation to prophesy are not individual matters. The Church is not a convention of independent, separate but equal messiahs. Neither are we the Church because we are by training or charism a special gnostic group. We are a gathering, an "event," if you will, of the great gathering, the *ekklesia*. Our wholeness, our authenticity depend on our unity with the *katholike*, the Church that reaches back to the apostles and to the Lord. It is the Church that is one in faith, holy in vocation, and apostolic in character and struggle. It is the Church of the tradition of the apostles that has "seen the Lord" and is able to be sure of his abiding presence. It is the Church that is the reality of life and hope in which we have reason to celebrate. It is to the Church that the Holy Spirit has been promised. It is the Church that is able to give a reason for its faith when men ask. It is the reality of the Church that makes it good for us to be here.

Permit me to try to make clear what I am saying. I know and can find no gathering of Christians, "institutional" or not, that believes and lives as does the Church Catholic, the Church in communion with the Holy Father and the College of Bishops. I know no other gathering of men that speaks any longer in terms of certainty. I know no way of life, no community other than the Church which offers a rational defense for its position and enables me to be a believer while remaining a rational man.

I feel that there has been rarely in history a moment when all of this is as important as it is now. *Commonweal* said recently in an editorial about the new Papal Creed that the Church has left the Pope behind. I for one do not want to leave him, for I know no other sign and source of unity. I rejoice to be a Catholic Christian. I rejoice to belong to the Church that produced the documents of Vatican II. I cannot agree with those who say that the Pope has betrayed those documents. The faith that I find professed and proclaimed at Vatican II is for me the present stage of the articulation of the same faith that was professed at Nicaea and Chalcedon. With the same faith through which I rejoice in the Constitution on the Church in the Modern World, I rejoice in the teaching of the First Vatican Council on God and human reason. With the same faith which deepens as I read the document on the liturgy, I rejoice in what the Council of Trent teaches about transubstantiation and the eucharistic sacrifice. The very basis of the Council is the continuity of the Church, and I cannot call myself a consistent man if I accept this Council and deny those of the past. For that very reason, I cannot see that the Pope is "left behind" for reaffirming in his Creed the teachings of past Councils. To be a Catholic is to be a man of the whole Church, *then* as well as *now*, for *Catholic* is a temporal as well as a spatial term. To be a Catholic is to be grafted into this lasting and growing Church that is the planting of Christ. Only in it do I find light for my darkness, reason to believe, hope that makes it possible to go on.

Permit me to put this back into the context of the shape of the Eucharist that we are celebrating. Last spring there came forth from the Consilium for "following through on the sacred liturgy" a document on worship which was one of the most exciting pieces of theology I have ever read. I have always had a deep interest in the liturgical practices of the early Protestant reformers, and my first thought on reading this document was that Calvin and Luther were most likely dancing before the ark in sheer joy. It says everything

that I (and I suspect they) ever hoped to see an official pronouncement say about the theology and form of Christian worship. It
speaks of the primacy of the Word; it teaches the manifold presence
of Jesus in Word, sacrament, minister, and congregation. It speaks
of the necessity of faith and understanding in sacramental celebration. It demands the restoration of contemplative prayer in the act
of public worship. It is a thrilling document, and it is a document
of the Church; it reflects the life and mind of a growing, reforming,
burgeoning Church. And yet so few of us have read it or put it
into practice.

I do not see that there is time to experiment behind closed doors
when we are not tending the lamps of the world's light. All the
energy and concern of a group of Catholic Christians can and must
be given *now* to making present in the local church the faith and
fervor of the Church universal. Otherwise, we join the company of
those who write blood-curdling accounts of why they left the
Church as it "used to be" and do not notice what it is now. When
I look for charism, when I look for relevance, when I look for
"where the action is," I find nothing better than the Church, the
Pope's Church, our Church. That is why I rejoice to be able to use
the form which the Church itself gives me to celebrate the life which
is mine because I am part of the Church.

I feel that it is this protest of unity with the Church that is the
grace of the moment; I feel that those who are "hanging loose" are
in danger of losing a great deal. It seems to me that the identity
crisis is what is expressed in the privately created liturgy. The Papal
Creed was a blow to many; the encyclical *Mysterium fidei* was
treated by some as Nasser might have been treated in Tel-Aviv during the six-day war in June, 1967. And yet, once again, without the
basis of Catholic tradition, we are without a consistent and defensible theology. Even in relation to the Eucharist itself, were it not for
the faith of the Church reaffirmed in *Mysterium fidei*, we would not
believe that it is the Lord Himself whom we encounter in the sacrament. It is as part of the "package" of the Church's faith that we can
know the joy of eucharistic celebration. It is in the light and strength
of the Church's faith that we have something to celebrate. We cannot pick and choose, for that is the meaning of *haeresis*, separation
from the mind and consequently from the Body that is the Church.
I fear that it is this which is about us today; I fear it is this which
is symbolized by private liturgies. Again, it is for this reason that I
feel that we should use the Church's own texts.

I have made frequent use of the word *tradition*. I would ask you not to place that term into a column marked "conservative" in the contemporary sense. I do not think it is fair to surrender tradition to the "traditionalists" as they are presently defined. I am not asking you to celebrate the thirteenth as the greatest of centuries. I am not glorifying the vision of those who think that authentic Christian practice is what they knew from 1870 Rome or in 1925 Brooklyn. I am asking you to take a serious look at the whole process that the living Church is and at its condition *now*. I am asking you to see that the Church Catholic *now*, in its mind and in its expressions of life in liturgy, is increasingly alive. I am asking you to look at a living Church in which, I suggest, you will be surprised by joy. I am asking you to look as intelligent men and women to see if there is any group of Christians in the world today which has more possibility of life and more consistency of intellectual vision than the Catholic community. In that sense, I am asking you to be phenomenologists of the Spirit. If you see as I do the dynamic of real reform and renewal in the unity of the visible Church, then I ask you to join with me in this Eucharist, which, by using the Church's own chosen method of worship, manifests our fellowship in that unity and commits us to dedicating our talent and energy to the ongoing process of the Church's growth and reform. We must, once again, not hide from the Church but rather act *as* the Church, *in* the Church, for the working out of the new creation of which the Church is the beginning.

The faith of the Church is a consistent vision; the life of the Church is a rational position; the worship of the Church is an expression, a celebration of all this. It is into the Church's life and vision that you were called in Baptism; it is from the Church's vision that I fear many are now receding. It is to share with you my own conviction of the truth of the Church's vision that I invite you into this celebration of the Eucharist. It is to manifest my own commitment to the visible Church that I insist the form of this Eucharist will be that of the Church itself.

I am speaking to you, quite obviously, in the context of what has happened around us within the last few months. As I have mentioned already, the reaction of many to the Papal Creed was very serious. The recent reaction to the encyclical on human life was even more traumatic. In both documents, Pope Paul calls us to unity. He echoes the admonition of the first Paul that we should "all say the same thing." I think it highly significant that the very man who

has most vocally defended the abandonment of the rather manu-
factured unity of a Latin liturgy and the ritual remoteness of a
service celebrated entirely by the clergy has issued such a clarion
call for deep unity in faith and in discipline within the Church. It
is a time to be at one in the way that counts, in the one faith that is
obedience to the one Lord in the fellowship of one Baptism. We
have left behind childlike expressions of unity and "safety" that were
necessary in the Counterreformation.

Again, let me speak of liturgy as a symptom of life. We celebrate
in our own language; we have a lectionary that places before us
the challenge of almost the entire Bible in our daily services; we
have the restoration of the cup to the laity. These are signs of life
and of maturity. But we need to see them in the context of the
other signs of this life and this maturation process that are part of
the same thrust of the Spirit in the Church. The life that we celebrate in the renewed liturgy is the same life that is manifest in the
encyclical *Humanae vitae*. I know of no document which speaks of
the dignity of human love as trustingly and warmly as it does. I
rejoice mightily at the theology of growth and of the use of the
sacraments as sources of strength for growth that it espouses. I can
imagine no more ringing reaffirmation of the faith of a Church that
is one throughout history than the Papal Creed. Yet it is these two
documents that are most attacked at this moment; and it is these
documents, which I heartily and firmly accept, that lead some to say
the Pope is behind the Church and the liturgical forms he is begging
us to use are expressions of that backwardness. It is because I can in
conscience stand in no other place than the one where he stands
that I use the Church's own liturgy in this celebration.

We are not a Church of religious geniuses. The Gospels show
us that, and the first letter to Corinth presents us with the theology
of the fact. We are a Church that began with a group of fishermen,
and as I see the names of so many of our scholars on protests against
the Pope, I begin to wonder if we are not fast returning to our
original condition. I fear very deeply to question the many good
and committed men who are involved in the protest against the
encyclical, just as I fear to question the fervent and holy men who
celebrate some of the experimental Eucharists that I have seen. But
I cannot find certitude in the principles from which they begin. I do
find certitude in the unity of the Church and the faith of the Church
as it is presented by the magisterium. It is that unity which for me
is the reality we celebrate in the Eucharist.

We celebrate in communion a fellowship of "knowledge and faith and life immortal" that courses from Jesus into His Body. His Body as I understand it is held together by the structural elements of hierarchical ministry and given the light of truth by their charism to teach. Our Eucharist is their Eucharist. I invite you to celebrate it in fervor and in faith. I invite you to see the problem of reform now as the reform of our hearts and minds. I invite you to pour into the words of the liturgy that we use over and over again the meaning and dedication that must be always new.

And since this Eucharist is the consecration of a new year of your work as teachers, I ask you to take the unity of the Body that we celebrate here and translate it in the ministry of your classrooms. What Jesus is to us in this Eucharist, what we are as the Church at Eucharist, let all this be continued in your mission to the young. The unity of the Church, the faith of the Church, the life of Jesus in the Church—these are the greatest gifts of God to man. It is these gifts of which you can make the young conscious as you teach them.

Do none of this underground. Be the light on the lamp stand; be the epiphany of Christ Jesus. Be, in the unity of a living and growing Church, a gathered and courageous cloud of witnesses. When you hear once again the words of the eucharistic prayer, "In union with the whole Church we honor the memory of the saints," remember that together with them you are bringing Jesus and His new creation into the world. It is in Him and in the strength of the rock upon which His Church is built that you have light to give. It is in Him that you have life; it is in His Church that you can choose life; it is in this Eucharist that we celebrate life. Let it be so. Amen.

Contributors

Contributors

PETER G. AHR did his undergraduate work at Seton Hall University, where he received his bachelor's degree in classical languages. He subsequently pursued graduate studies in theology at the University of Innsbruck, and returned to Seton Hall as an instructor in theology. Further studies in theology took him to Saint Michael's College at the University of Toronto, for which he is now completing his doctoral dissertation on the Greek Fathers' exegesis of John's Gospel. He is presently an assistant professor of theology at Seton Hall University, and has published several theological articles, as well as translations in the two volumes *The Church: Readings in Theology* (New York, Kenedy, 1963) and *The Word: Readings in Theology* (New York, Kenedy, 1964).

T. PATRICK BURKE studied at the University of Queensland and continued at the University of Munich, where he received his doctorate in theology. He has taught in the School of Religion at the State University of Iowa, and was affiliated with the Department of Theology at Saint Xavier College in Chicago. Also in Chicago, he was director of the John XXIII Institute. Professor Burke has been a visiting lecturer in theology at the Catholic University of America, and is now teaching in the Department of Religion at Temple University. He is the author of *Faith and the Human Person* (Chicago, John XXIII Institute, 1968) and the editor of the symposium *Word in History* (New York, Sheed & Ward, 1966) and of Michael Schmaus's *Manual of Doctrinal Theology* in six volumes, being published by Sheed & Ward. He also has many theological articles to his credit.

SISTER ANITA CASPARY, I.H.M., received her bachelor's degree from Immaculate Heart College, her master's from the University of Southern California, and her doctorate from Stanford University, and has pursued postdoctoral studies at the University of California at Los Angeles. She was chairman of the English Department of Immaculate Heart College, then dean of the Graduate School, and later president, simultaneously holding positions on the Board of Trustees and Board of Regents of the College as well as the General Council of the Immaculate Heart Sisters. From 1963 to the present she has been Mother General of the California Institute of the Sisters of the Immaculate Heart of Mary, a pontifical institute. A leader in education and a member of many academic groups, Sister Anita has published in a variety of journals and volumes.

JOHN B. COBB, JR., began his education at Emory University and the University of Michigan, later receiving his master's and doctor's degrees from the University of Chicago Divinity School. An ordained Methodist minister, he taught at Young Harris Junior College in Georgia, and was a member of the faculty of the Candler School of Theology and the Graduate School at Emory University. He is presently Ingraham Professor of Theology in the School of Theology at Claremont, California. His books include *Varieties of Protestantism* (Philadelphia, Westminster, 1960), *Living Options in Protestant Theology* (Philadelphia, Westminster, 1962), *A Christian Natural Theology* (Philadelphia, Westminster, 1965), and *The Structure of Christian Existence* (Philadelphia, Westminster, 1967). He has also edited several volumes and authored myriad articles.

JOHN COGLEY received his bachelor's degree from Loyola University in Chicago, and did graduate study in philosophy at the University of Fribourg. Since serving in the United States Air Force during World War II, he has had a varied and interesting career, having been editor of *Today* magazine and a contributing editor to the periodical *Commonweal*. For some years he was associate director of the Fund for the Republic, and he was a special assistant in the successful 1960 presidential campaign of John F. Kennedy. More recently he served as religious news editor of *The New York Times,* and received an award from the Catholic Press Association for his coverage of the third session of Vatican Council II. Presently Mr. Cogley is associated with the Center for the Study of

Democratic Institutions in Santa Barbara, California. Needless to say, he has published extensively.

GEORGE DEVINE received his bachelor's degree from the University of San Francisco and his master's in theology from Marquette University. He has taught theology at Marquette and at Seton Hall University, where he currently holds the rank of assistant professor. Author of *Our Living Liturgy* and *Why Read the Old Testament?* (Chicago, Claretian Publications, 1966), he has published articles in *Worship, U.S. Catholic,* and *Christian Art,* of which he was associate editor for several years. He is also liturgical music columnist for *The Advocate* (Newark), and lectures extensively. Professor Devine specializes in liturgy, and has devised and led programs of lay involvement in the liturgy in various parts of the United States for more than a decade.

REV. ROBERT L. FARICY, S.J., is a graduate of the United States Naval Academy, and pursued studies in education and philosophy at Saint Louis University and in theology at the Séminaire de Missions in Lyons, France. He received his degree of doctor of sacred theology from the Catholic University of America, where he is now an assistant professor in the Religious Education Department and the director of the University's Commission on American Citizenship. Father Faricy is the author of *Teilhard de Chardin's Theology of the Christian in the World* (New York, Sheed & Ward, 1967), and of articles in such journals as *New Scholasticism, Theological Studies, Theology Today, Review for Religious, American Ecclesiastical Review,* and *Sisters Today.*

JOHN A. HUTCHISON received his bachelor of science degree from Lafayette College, his bachelor of divinity from Union Theological Seminary, and his doctorate from Columbia University. He was also a student at the University of Basel and the University of Edinburgh. An ordained minister of the Presbyterian Church, he has been assistant pastor of Brown Memorial Church in Baltimore and pastor of Christ Church in Bayonne, New Jersey. His teaching career includes an instructorship in philosophy at the College of Wooster, Ohio, where he was later professor of religion, and professorships in religion at Williams College and Columbia University; since 1960 he has been Danforth Professor of the Philosophy of Religion at the Claremont Graduate School in Claremont, California. He has written a number of books, and is a member of the Society on Religion in Higher Education, the Society for Biblical Literature, and Phi Beta Kappa.

REV. CHARLES KOHLI is a priest of the Diocese of Rockville Centre, Long Island, New York, having been ordained at Immaculate Conception Seminary in Huntington, Long Island. His studies led to the degree of bachelor of sacred theology from the Catholic University of America. He has taught at Molloy College in Rockville Centre, particularly in adult education, and also in the College Extension of Alphonsus College in Woodcliff Lake, New Jersey. Father Kohli specializes in New Testament studies, and lectures extensively in addition to his priestly assignment at Saint Patrick's Church in Glen Cove, Long Island.

ROBERT MICHAELSEN holds a bachelor of arts degree from Cornell University, a bachelor of divinity from Yale University Divinity School, and a doctorate from Yale University Graduate School. As a Methodist minister, he has been pastor in Waregan and Central Village, Connecticut. In the academic sphere, he has been an assistant professor in the School of Religion at the State University of Iowa, a Ford Foundation faculty fellow at Harvard University, an assistant professor of American Christianity in the Yale University Divinity School, and a professor in the School of Religion at the State University of Iowa. Since 1965, he has served as professor and chairman of the Department of Religious Studies of the University of California at Santa Barbara. He is the author of *The Study of Religion in American Universities: Ten Case Studies with Special Reference to State Universities* (New Haven, The Society for Religion in Higher Education, 1965), and of theological articles in a variety of journals.

JACK VAUGHN earned his bachelor's and master's degrees at the University of Michigan, and also studied at the University of Pennsylvania and the National University of Mexico. He was head boxing coach at the University of Michigan, and later an instructor there and at the University of Pennsylvania. After being director of Overseas Information Centers in Bolivia and Costa Rica for the United States Information Agency, he worked with the International Cooperation Administration, and was assigned to Bolivia, Panama, and Guinea, serving also as representative to Senegal. Afterwards he was detailed to the faculty of the School of Advanced International Studies at Johns Hopkins University.

Mr. Vaughn was regional director of the Peace Corps for Latin America and United States ambassador to Panama as well as co-ordinator of the Alliance for Progress prior to his 1966 appointment as director of the Peace Corps.

REV. THOMAS A. WASSMER, S.J., received his higher education through his doctorate at Fordham University, his licentiate in philosophy from Woodstock College, and his licentiate in sacred theology from Weston College in Massachusetts. He has served on the theological faculty of Saint Peter's College, and was recently a scholar in residence at the Episcopal Theological School in Cambridge, Massachusetts, assisting Dr. Joseph Fletcher in his classes in Christian ethics. Since September, 1968, Father Wassmer has been professor of moral philosophy at Ohio University. He has published a great number of scholarly articles in the fields of philosophy and theology in the United States, Europe, Canada, and Australia, and is presently putting finishing touches on a book on Christian ethics.

VINCENT ZAMOYTA holds a bachelor's degree from the Catholic University of America and three master of arts degrees: one in theology from Saint John's University in New York, one in philosophy from the Catholic University of America, and one in education from Seton Hall University. He received his doctorate in philosophy from the Catholic University of America, and is now completing studies toward a doctorate in theology at Fordham University. Formerly in the Department of Theology at Seton Hall University, he is now associate professor of theology at Saint John's University. Professor Zamoyta is the author of *A Theology of Christ: Sources* (Milwaukee, Bruce, 1967) and has penned a number of articles. He is on the Editorial Advisory Committee of the Brooklyn diocesan newspaper, *The Tablet*, and recently received a grant from the Association for Research and Experimentation in Higher Education to offer an experimental course in theology at Saint John's University.